In *They Call Me Dad*, Phillip Cameron writes a mo love the abandoned, hurting children in Romania. journey enabling his ministry to provide safe ar and loving guidance for teenage girls in dangerous Romania, Moldova, and other countries. This book is a must read and will change your life. It will re-fire your passion for missions and for the plight of less fortunate, children in need of an earthly dad who can lead them to the Father's love.

Marcus D. Lamb, Founder—President Daystar Television Network

If the passion of a man is truly a reflection of the God-given heart of that man, then Philip Cameron's heart is infinite in its capacity. His heart for children continues to expand beyond reason and limits. The theme of his life has been "give me a heart for others." I have personally witnessed his passion and unlimited love for the neglected and forgotten children of this world. When I saw Philip's vision firsthand, I knew we had to help him make it happen. Stella's House was birthed from that desire and heart for others. Thank you, Philip, for making the world a better and brighter place for thousands of children and for those of us who witness that miracle of love.

Dr. Garth W. Coonce, President / TCT Network

I'm so excited that Philip has finally written the book *They Call Me Dad*. It's the incredible story of how Stella's Voice began with one man, and yet transformed the lives of hundreds of young people who literally had no hope. After reading this book, you'll never doubt what can be achieved by a single, committed individual again.

**—Phil Cooke, filmmaker, media consultant,
and author of *One Big Thing: Discovering What You Were Born to Do***

When you read the stories of these girls and how God has transformed them completely, you will realize that this is a miracle in our current generation. In the challenges of the world we live in today, this is an unprecedented story of the grace and mercy of God. You will laugh and you will cry, but you will never be the same!

**—Bishop Paul D. Zink, Founder,
New Life Christian Fellowship and Providence School**

God called my friend "with the huge heart" to Moldova to rescue children who had been thrown into the garbage heaps of humanity. Philip has been faithful to that call. You will love his story contained in this remarkable book.

—**Dan Betzer, First Assembly of God, Ft. Myers, Florida**

By being a "dad" to kids who are orphaned out of state-run facilities where they have been abused and abandoned, Philip is showing how the Love of Christ in action can change lives. Once you meet these young men and women, you are overwhelmed by their stories and how much their lives have been changed by the power of Christ and this ministry!

—**David Byrnes, Founder/CEO, FACTS Management Co,
Chairman of the Board, Monmouth College**

"Pure and undefiled religion before God and the Father is this: to visit orphans and widows in their trouble, and to keep oneself unspotted from the world" (James 1:27). This real-life story of caring for the completely helpless literally half-way around the world is what this scripture looks like. And one of the things I appreciate most about Phillip's recounting is his honesty in telling how he did not want to get involved, how he felt that these children were not his responsibility. But he did get involved.

—**Jeff Patterson, Tax Attorney, Montgomery, Alabama**

This story is an inspiring example of the life-changing love of God and the things that can be accomplished when God's servants are obedient, even reluctantly so, to His voice.

—**Glenn B. Cooke, CEO, Cooke Aquaculture Inc.**

They Call Me Dad exemplifies a masterpiece of God's divine planning in the lives of people. From a persistent plea of a critically ill father to the forgotten live television interview to the fox that mysteriously appeared on the road, God's divine plan is vividly portrayed to an often unknowing preacher. This is a must read for those struggling as life's path is full of obstacles and questions.

—**Dr. Dawn R. Butler, Assistant Professor of Education,
Huntingdon College, Montgomery, Alabama**

I have witnessed some of this book while it was happening and have seen God's love in Philip and Chrissie grow to become Stella's Voice. As a businessman and the father of seven children, I can promise you that anyone would benefit from reading *They Call Me Dad,* and every person should. Philip Cameron is uniquely qualified and anointed to write about and to demonstrate Abba Father!!!

—Peter F. Welden, Co-Founder and CEO of Jubilee Donuts, Inc.
Board Member, Stella's Voice

This book masterfully tells the compelling story of a man who has sacrificed much in order to be a father to so many. Hopefully it will inspire others to follow in his footsteps.

—Jay Stewart (JayStewart.tv),
Founding/Lead Pastor of The Refuge in the greater Charlotte area, and
author of *The Ultimate Road Trip: 12 Journeys that Shape Your Future*

This story will inspire you, grip you and challenge you to join Philip and the Stella's Voice team as they work tirelessly to change lives. This is more than a great story that must be told, the very heart of God is seen in Philip's determination to save these lost children!

—John Greenow, Pastor, Xcel church, UK

I was deeply moved by Philip Cameron's story. Not only is it a page turner, but it has forced me to ponder my own life. The author gave me a glimpse into the incredible blessings God is waiting to bestow on His followers when they wholeheartedly obey Him. I've been challenged to live that level of obedience and discover that level of blessing.

—Jill Jones, Milford, New Hampshire, Pastor's Wife

They Call Me Dad is a living illustration of redemption and restoration. We pray that as you read this book, you would allow the Father's love to do the same in you.

—Rusty & Leisa Nelson, Lead Pastors of
The Rock Family Worship Center, Huntsville, Alabama

They Call Me Dad is a "must read"! Written by my dear friend Philip Cameron, this book will take you on an incredible journey that has the power to center you again on what really matters—people! Once you start reading you will have great trouble putting this book down. In it you will experience the very Father heart of God. Read, be challenged, then arise and do something about it.

—Andy Elmes, Pastor of Family Church, Portsmouth, England

An emotionally inspiring, humbling and life-changing story. *They Call Me Dad* not only captures Philip's personal story so far, but it also shines a light on the biggest crime of our day and age—human trafficking.

—Phil Jones, Managing Director, Heinz UK&I

In *They Call Me Dad*, Philip tells the story of his courageous efforts to build houses for these children who have been abandoned and preyed upon by relatives, bureaucrats, and sex traffickers. These children may call Philip "Dad," but I call him the William Wallace of east Europe's orphans.

**—Ben DuPré, Attorney and Chief of Staff to
Chief Justice Roy Moore, Alabama Supreme Court**

Philip couldn't stop crying and talking about what he had just seen. It was a Christmas get together with our wives, but there was little Christmas joy. Philip had just returned from seeing for the first time the tragic orphan situation in Moldova, and something had to be done. *They Call Me Dad* is the faith-filled journey of Philip and Stella's Voice from a night of tears to tears of joy. You may shed a tear when you read the story of all the changed lives of young men and women who call him Dad.

—Pastor Mike Rippy, Evangel Church, Montgomery, Alabama

PHILIP CAMERON

THEY CALL ME DAD

HOW GOD USES THE UNLIKELY TO SAVE THE DISCARDED

HIGHERLIFE
PUBLISHING & MARKETING, INC.
Oviedo, Florida

They Call Me Dad, How God Uses the Unlikely to Save the Discarded
By Philip Cameron

Scripture marked NASB is taken from the NEW AMERICAN STAN-
DARD BIBLE®, Copyright © 1960, 1962, 1963, 1968, 1971, 1972, 1973,
1975, 1977, 1995 by The Lockman Foundation. Used by permission.

Scripture marked NIV is taken from THE HOLY BIBLE, NEW INTER-
NATIONAL VERSION®, NIV® Copyright © 1973, 1978, 1984, 2011
by Biblica, Inc.™ Used by permission. All rights reserved worldwide.

Scripture marked KJV is taken from the King James Version of the Bible.

Published by HigherLife Publishing and Marketing
400 Fontana Circle Building 1, Suite 105
Oviedo, Florida 32765
(407) 563-4806
www.ahigherlife.com

ISBN Paperback: 978-1-939183-21-7
ISBN Hardback: 978-1-939183-31-6
ISBN e-book: 978-1-939183-22-4

Cover Design: Doni Keene
keene-ideas.com

Printed in the United States of America

TABLE OF CONTENTS

THE BABIES ARE DYING

It was February, one of my favorite times of the year in Alabama. There was no need for air-conditioning or heat, and signs of flowers just starting to bud were everywhere. My short drive home from the office was lovely.

I pulled into the driveway, climbed out of my car, and slowly made my way to the door, taking in a deep breath of the pleasant air. Southern Alabama was nothing like the wet, raw climate of Scotland, where I was raised. I loved the feeling.

Chrissie was busy in the kitchen when I passed through the foyer, and the smell of roast beef and potatoes filled the air. After greeting her with a quick kiss on the cheek, I headed to the back bedroom, kicked off my loafers, and quickly changed my clothes. I was more than ready to settle in front of the television set in my easy chair and numb the day's happenings with *The Cosby Show* or *Matlock* as soon as the news was over.

From down the hall, I could hear the faint sound of music coming from one of the kids' rooms. A dog could be heard barking up the street. It was a normal evening in 1990 in the Cameron household. After stepping over a few of the kids' toys, I settled into my chair. As I popped up the footrest, the clock on the mantel struck 5:30, and the evening news with Peter Jennings filled the screen. Then, the phone rang.

The shrill ringing rose above all of the other commotion in the house, demanding attention like a toothache.

I stared at the receiver beside me and held my breath for a second, wanting the phone to stop ringing and my blood pressure not to rise. It wasn't the phone itself that was the problem. The problem was I knew who was calling, and I knew what he was going to say. Chrissie poked her head around the door to make sure I was by the phone and would answer it. "Yes," the look on my face said as I nodded, "I will answer. But I don't want to."

> "Philip, are you there?" he started again. "Did you hear me? Babies are dying, and you have to do something!"

Ring! Ring!

"Hel—"

"Philip," I heard before I could finish saying hello, "babies are dying."

The voice belonged to my beloved father, Simon Cameron. Dad was one of the greatest preachers, evangelists, and worship leaders of his day. I loved him more than life itself, but his recent calls were driving me crazy.

At 66 years of age, he had a recent surgery to remove cancer from his back, leaving him housebound in Scotland. Other than my mother, the only company he had was an aged Sylvania television set that was turned to the news around the clock.

For a man who was used to being busy nonstop with ministry, the bed rest was hard to take. Half a world away, he was starting to watch the same newscast I was watching, but it was all he thought about, all he could talk about. And the lead story on every newscast

2

was that abandoned babies were dying in Eastern Europe, especially in Romania.

The fall of Communism had come only months before. The iron curtain was finally destroyed, and detailed news from the Soviet Bloc was finally being reported to the outside world. Before the fall, no one in the Western world knew that mass orphanages, filled with babies living in horrible conditions, littered these countries. Suddenly, these children were featured on one television news report after the other. My dad had had a steady diet of these reports for days, and he was like a man possessed; nothing else seemed to matter to him.

"Philip, are you there?" he started again. "Did you hear me? Babies are dying, and you have to do something!"

I heard him moan in pain as he shifted in the chair. "Philip," he said before he started to weep.

From the corner of my eye, I could see Chrissie starting to set the dining room table. She'd be calling the kids, nine year-old Philip Jr. and eight year-old Melody, down any minute. I was tired and hungry and had heard the same plea from my dad every night for a week. I kept thinking that as he began to heal, he'd start reading or writing— doing anything other than watching these blasted news reports. This obsession had to stop, or he would make both of us crazy.

"Dad, I love you, but you need to hear me. You are very, very sick. You need rest. You need to turn off the television and go to sleep. If you don't rest, you can't heal. Please. Go to bed. Let's talk tomorrow," I said as I scooted forward in my chair and started to get up. Chrissie caught my eye, and I signaled that I would be with her at the table in just a moment.

There was silence on the other end of the phone. I thought the matter was finally closed.

"Philip. Listen to me. These babies are starving to death. They are warehoused in these buildings with no one to care for them. Hundreds of them. Dying. You must do something!"

The shadow of reports out of Romania rattled in the back of my mind. A horrible man by the name of Nicolae Ceaușescu, the dictator at the time, wanted to double the population of his country in a decade's time. He outlawed birth control and required every married couple to produce at least five children. The results were nightmarish.

With the explosion of birth rates in Romania, the little available food there had been was long gone. People were starving. By the thousands, babies and toddlers were left at the doors of state-run orphanages, their parents disappearing into the night.

It was tragic, no doubt about it. But it wasn't my tragedy. It was half a world away in a country I had never even visited, and rarely thought of, until my dad started this nonsense.

"This is the kind of problem governments solve—the Red Cross, The Salvation Army. The big boys handle problems like these," I tried to explain.

After listening to him ramble on for a few more moments, I'd had enough. How could I possibly help these babies from my living room in southern Alabama? "Dad, I have to go. Chrissie has dinner ready, and the kids are just sitting down at the table," I said. "Please, go to bed. I love you. Good night."

With both of us frustrated, I hung up and walked over to the table. Philip Jr. was already helping himself to the potatoes, while Melody was making faces at me. These were the only children I needed to worry about, had time to worry about.

I was a busy man, traveling across the country preaching the gospel in churches, on Christian television, at conferences, and at retreats. My ministry took me away from my family too much already.

God had blessed my ministry in ways that amazed me. Clearly, I was in the center of His will; how else could I explain it? People were getting saved everywhere I went. Long-lost relatives for whom I had prayed were coming back to Jesus. Scores were being healed; lives were being changed. It was all good, so very good.

Life was finally the way it was supposed to be. After years of living hand to mouth, dragging my wife and firstborn child all over the country in an RV—the first home we owned—I enjoyed the lovely house in which we now lived. I liked driving the well-used, but well-loved, Mercedes-Benz instead of the rattletrap I'd had for years.

I had it all: ministry, family, security. Everything was good except my dad and those pesky phone calls. My mood ruined, I went to bed early in a pout and hoped the next day would be better.

Starting early the next morning, I put in a full day at my office making plans for some upcoming meetings. Over the recent years, God had anointed me to speak on the subject of household salvation, and the results had been amazing everywhere I went, making me a sought-after guest on Christian television.

As soon as I got home, tired again, but excited about my upcoming trip, the phone started ringing.

Ring! Ring!

"Philip. Babies are dying. What are you going to do about it?"

Still in my work clothes, I stood there at my wit's end. I was in no mood for this. "Look, Dad, you are sick. I am busy. Leave this alone."

Before I got the words out, he was back at me: "That's easy for you to say, my boy. If they were your babies, you would do something!"

"But Dad, that's the point," I said, trying to calm down. "They are not my babies."

He let out a sigh. I knew that sound. I had him. I finally had him agreeing with me! Now I could eat dinner with my family without a load of guilt hanging over my head.

I was about to say good-bye when he said, "Okay, fine. Then I'll go. If you won't do something about these babies, I will. I can't turn my back on this. I can't. So if you won't go, I will." He paused for just a moment and then continued, "And if I die on the trip, it will be your fault."

He let that sink in. I tried to argue, but what more could I say? I couldn't let my dad get in a car and go to Romania any more than I could let him fly to the moon. He was too sick, too frail. He was right; the trip would kill him. But he'd do it; he would make the trip, and no one or nothing would stop him. The battle was over. I had lost. I was going to Romania.

The rest of the evening was a blur. I was mad, frustrated, and looking for a target to take my frustrations out on. I barked loudly enough to clear the kids and my wife out of the living room and settled into my chair. I wanted to be alone so I could pout some more.

Leaving home was always hard for me. I loved being with my wife and family. I had everything a man could ask for. "Well, I'll do this to get my dad off my back," I told myself. "Then I can get back to real life." So, I'd make the trip first to Scotland to pick up Dad, then overseas to Romania; punch the clock, as they say; and hurry back to Alabama.

The next morning, I drove to work thinking about the ramifications of the sudden trip. One pastor would be fine with rescheduling my planned visit, but the other would be upset, possibly never ask me to speak at his church again. Then there was the camp meeting to which I was supposed to fly. I had a headache just thinking about all the calls, the reactions, the impact this could have on my ministry in the future.

> There were times when it almost seemed like he left his body and was one with the Father.

I pulled into the parking lot of the office at the same time as Lisa Crews, the ministry's financial manager. She would not be happy when I asked her to book my flight to Scotland and cancel all my other ones for two weeks. This last-minute trip would be costly.

Despite my worries, by noon it was all taken care of, and two days later, I boarded a British Airways jet and settled in for the overnight flight. Believe me, there is no comfortable way to sleep on those planes, especially for a big guy like me. Irritated anew, I grabbed a few extra pillows and commandeered the empty seat beside me. *Thank God for small favors,* I thought.

I closed my eyes, and my mind immediately wandered to what was ahead of me in Scotland: my dad. I loved him so much. He was the finest man I knew. I had learned so much from him about being a man, a husband, a father, and a soul-winner. He taught by example, always being fair, Christ-centered, and kind.

Sure, I was annoyed at him about this trip, but I was worried too. As much as I hated to admit it, it would be good to see him, talk to Mom and the doctors, and see if anything more could be done to promote his healing. After the cancer had been removed, his healing had not gone as well as we'd hoped. The operation left a hole as big as a fist in his back, and it became infected, causing him much pain and suffering.

It was hard for me to wrap my head around the concept of my dad being sick. He had an amazing relationship with God. He talked to God, and God talked to him. There were times when it almost seemed like he left his body and was one with the Father.

Nibbling on the tasteless sandwich that the flight attendant placed in front of me, I decided that when I arrived I would show my dad the respect he deserved. No matter how silly his notion for us to go to Romania was, I would listen, be patient, and perhaps finally talk some sense into him.

The hours dragged by; I slept little on the plane. When I finally arrived in Scotland, I gathered my bags and stepped out into the cold winter air. My jacket, which had been fine in Alabama, was not quite heavy enough.

As I started toward my parents' house, I found myself anxious to see Dad. During the hour-long drive from the airport, I shook the cobwebs out of my brain as the road took me past the familiar sights of my youth. I decided I would visit with Dad and Mom, have a cup of tea and a bite to eat, and then take a nice long nap. Handling the whole "babies are dying" matter would be much easier once my batteries were recharged.

But as I pulled onto Dad's property, I was surprised to see an unusual whirlwind of activity. There were cars and trucks coming and going, all of them unloading huge boxes and bags filled with things.

"What the heck is going on here?" I asked no one in particular, looking around for someone I knew—a sibling, a cousin, someone who worked with my folks. Where was someone who could tell me what the devil was going on here? What were all of those overstuffed plastic bags? What was in those boxes? Where had all this stuff come from? And what was it for?

It didn't take long to figure it out. My dad had been quite busy from his "sickbed." Apparently, he had made calls to every pastor, every friend, and every other person he knew in Scotland about his upcoming trip. The local newspaper even carried the following headline the day before I arrived: "Cancer-Stricken Pastor to Go to Romania."

So, on top of the food, clothing, and medical donations that poured in from people he knew, now total strangers were arriving with goods. The local Salvation Army gave him a truckload of diapers and supplies. The Red Cross donated baby bottles, formula, and food. Crosse & Blackwell, a giant food production company, brought five tons of canned goods. Another company gave cases and cases of oranges. People who had seen the same news stories Dad watched had come from miles and miles around. I had never seen more coats, blankets, food, and baby items in all my life.

It all seemed wonderful. Being the practical one in the bunch, I could only focus on one thing: How, for the love of God, would we get all this stuff to Romania, two thousand miles away?

Dad had small panel trucks that he used for ministry work, but nothing like what it would require to transport all of this. Only a much larger truck would hold all of these goods, but no one we knew had one of those just sitting in the driveway.

With my planned tea and nap forgotten, I went into the house for a quick visit with Dad before getting down to business. Never mind trying to talk Dad out of going; there was no fighting it now. I didn't know how, but I knew we were going to Romania.

When I walked into his room, Dad was sitting up in an overstuffed chair, leaning forward so his sore back didn't touch the cushion. With the base of the phone between his legs, he screamed into the other end of it something about packing crates.

As he finished the conversation, I tried to take in everything around me. Beside Dad's well-worn Bible, a row of pill bottles lined the nightstand. He'd lost a lot of weight since I'd seen him last, and his face was a bit ashen, his color off because of the infection. But his eyes danced with excitement. I knew that look well. Anytime my dad was moving toward a miracle, he had an unmistakable glow that no sickness could dim. I smiled in spite of myself.

Romania. Two thousand miles away. I would find out soon that in this country of 22 million people, there were 104,000 orphans in state-run institutions. I also would learn that what I considered a road and what Communist countries considered a road were two completely different things. I was in for a very long and hard trip, but I was blissfully unaware of these details.

After a short visit, I went down to Dad's office, pulled out a legal pad and phone book, and started the process of locating a truck. I was both shocked and pleased when the first man I called agreed at once to lease a truck to me.

It was all perfect. Too perfect.

"Just one thing," the man finished: "I need you to wire me a $100,000 deposit."

I was sure that with my overtired brain, I had misunderstood him. "Excuse me? $100,000? You must have misunderstood. I want to lease the truck, not buy it," I said.

9

"Mr. Cameron," the man replied, now talking to me in a tone often used with a dull-minded child, "Romania is a war zone. If my truck is going to be taken into a war zone, I must insure it."

My heart sank. This was not going to be easy. I looked out the window. More cars and trucks. More little pink blankets, cans of food, baby clothes. How the heck would I get all of this to Romania?

I hung up and started down the next listings in the phone book. Over and over, I heard the words, "Sorry, we can't help you" as soon as the word "Romania" was out of my mouth. I'd hang up, dial the next number, and repeat my then well-rehearsed speech: "Hi, my name is Philip Cameron. I assume you have been watching the news lately about the tragic situation in Romania. There are babies dying there. I am a preacher, and we have gathered food, clothing, and blankets for these babies, but we still need to find a way to get these items there. We need a truck, a big truck. Can you help me?"

> His determination to help these babies was amazing, and I had neither the heart nor the guts to tell him that I still had not located a truck.

No one laughed at me, but after that $100,000 bombshell, no one said yes either. I was down to one last number, for a company called Clark and Rose.

I dialed the number, delivered my spiel, and braced myself for more bad news.

"I'll get back to you in an hour," the man said.

I was so surprised, I stammered out, "You will? You'll get back to me?"

After he assured me that he would call, we hung up, and I decided to go and check on my dad again. I found him on the phone, looking more tired but still yelling, a bit louder this time, into the phone. Some poor soul was being dressed down for not coming through with formula that had been promised. His determination to help these babies was amazing, and I had neither the heart nor the guts to tell him that I still had not located a truck.

Ten minutes passed, and he was still on the phone. I slowly turned and walked down the stairs, the steps creaking under my feet. I was so tired and so overwhelmed with a sense of helplessness. Feeling quite sorry for myself, I rounded the corner to the office just as the phone began to ring.

"Is this Philip Cameron?" the voice asked. "It is? Well, we have a furniture truck for you. We at Clark and Rose want to help these babies. If you will just pay for the fuel, you can borrow the truck for as long as you need."

I was dumbfounded, excited, over the moon. I couldn't wait to tell Dad! What a miracle! What a breakthrough! What a God!

CHAPTER 2

NO ORPHANAGES?

M Y PARENTS LIVED IN Peterhead, far into the northern part of Scotland. Looking at a map of Europe, you'll notice Peterhead is about the farthest point in the United Kingdom from Romania. Finding any maps to direct us from Scotland to Romania was a challenge, as eastern Europe had been closed to Westerners for decades.

It seemed straightforward enough, though: Go south, cross over into Belgium, and then go through Germany, east through Austria and Hungary, and finally into Romania. But we knew enough to know we had no clue what to expect.

At the end of our road trip, all we would have to go on was the name and address of a pastor in Timișoara, Romania. It was enough for my dad, so it had to be enough for me.

With the furniture truck stuffed so full that I was sure the sidewalls were bulging, we were off. My father, brother Neil, brother-in-law John Reid, and I led the caravan in a ragtag ambulance that we'd converted into a poor man's RV followed by a professional driver in the jam-packed truck.

We started out at dawn, bags of snacks and thermoses of tea in hand. I adjusted the seat and mirrors in the car for the long trip ahead, and glanced at my dad. The pain was evident on his face. Although my mom had made the bandages on his back thicker and softer to offer some comfort from the hard vinyl car seat, I knew they would provide little relief.

I also knew my dad well enough to know he would not complain no matter how much agony he was in. I'd drive the "ambulance" as carefully as I could, but this trip was going to be very hard for him. After I'd agreed to make the trip, my mom, siblings, and I had all tried to talk him out of going, but there was no stopping him. He was passionate about these kids he had never met, he had worked for weeks gathering all this stuff, and he was going to see it all delivered, even if it killed him. Literally.

We turned onto the A90 a short time later. When we circled around the roundabout, I saw that my dad had fallen asleep. Silently I prayed that he'd sleep for much of the trip; it would do him good. I turned on some worship music on the portable cassette player I'd carried along and let my mind drift.

As we traveled through England, past London and then took the ferry across the English Channel into Belgium, the roads passed through farmland and open fields, then through small villages that offered snapshots of what I pictured a bygone era to be.

Four days later, on a snowy Tuesday afternoon, we arrived in Romania. From the moment we crossed the border into Romania, we were struck by the sadness of the country. It was a country that had once been beautiful, filled with small, freshly painted houses with flower boxes on the windows and tidy lawns.

But Communism had long since broken this country. After World War II, the Soviets dealt harshly with the Romanian people. Thousands and thousands of people suspected of being enemies of Mother Russia were removed from their homes and shipped by train to the coal mines for up to ten years as "reparation" for their supposed crimes.

There were other worries for those who were left. The Communists went from one town to the next bulldozing the existing houses and replacing them with high-rise apartment-type buildings, each one as ugly and windowless as the one built before it. By design, several of these "filing cabinets" for humans ran off a single heating system. If there was trouble with a citizen in one building, the government would shut off the heat in all of the other buildings, making sure all the neighbors knew why. It wasn't long before the lone citizen would fall back into line.

The bulldozing process took time; every year a few thousand more houses would go down, and a few more high-rises would go up. The people who still had houses knew that it was only a matter of time before the bulldozers would be on their streets, so they stopped painting, stopped fixing the roofs.

> By the time Communism finally collapsed, the country had people living in two situations: either in the horrible high-rises, or in broken-down houses. There was nothing else left.

Years went by. Children in the generation grew up watching their parents live in houses that were slowly falling apart. It became normal. All the houses that were left were crumbling, their roofs sagging, and the paint chipping. No one fixed anything.

By the time Communism finally collapsed, the country had people living in two situations: either in the horrible high-rises, or in broken-down houses. There was nothing else left.

As I drove across the country that dark day in 1990, the people were free of the iron fist of the Soviet Union, but they were still in bondage. The economy had collapsed along with everything else; there was no money, no banking system. The people were left with more children than they could feed, useless educations, no jobs, and nothing and no one to look to for help. The government had been their only source for decades, and now it was gone.

Yes, it was a sad, sad country. While the roads along our journey had been bad, they were worse in Romania. The potholes were filled with dirty snow and ice, making it nearly impossible to see them in the light of dusk as we pulled into Timişoara. After a few U-turns and false starts, I finally found the small church we were searching for, and the pastor opened the door when we knocked.

Thankfully, he spoke enough English that we were able to communicate. "Hi, my name is Philip Cameron. This is my dad, Simon. I am hoping you can help me. We have been watching the news reports out of Romania, and we have seen the terrible condition of the orphanages. We want to help.

"In fact," I continued, pointing behind me, "we have a furniture truck loaded with supplies. We have food, medicine, diapers, clothes, and blankets. We just need some help. Can you direct us to the closest orphanage?"

His face was blank, completely blank. It was as though I had asked him where the nearest people with green skin lived.

Thinking perhaps he had not understood me, I repeated myself, more slowly and a little louder. I was met with the same blank stare as he shook his head.

"I don't know what you are talking about," he said. "There are no orphanages around here."

The country wasn't that large. I was stunned by what he was telling me. We were in one of the largest cities, talking to a man of the cloth, a man whose job would have been to know if the type of suffering I was talking about was anywhere near him.

"I am sorry. I have never even heard of there being orphanages around here," he continued. "Sure, there are children that are poor. We are all poor. But an orphanage with children who are dying? No."

No orphanages? The news was shocking and unwelcome. Here we were in a country we didn't know, tired to the bone with no backup plan, with Dad sicker than I wanted to believe.

In a country as desperate as post-Communist Romania, any gang of hoodlums would readily kill us to get ahold of the truckload of goods behind me. We had no names or addresses for the orphanages, and no idea where to go or what to do next. We didn't speak the language, so we had no way to get directions to a motel to sleep in that night.

"I have an idea," the pastor said, as though reading my mind. "Why don't you unload the truck into the church warehouse? We have sturdy locks, and the building is well-protected. I'll direct you to a motel, you can get a good night's sleep, and tomorrow I can help you make some calls to find the best way to help children."

With great relief, I nodded my head. It would only take a few hours at best to unload the truck, and I'd finally be able to sleep. Every bone in my body ached from being in the car for so long. While the pastor went and rounded up a few locals to help us unload the truck, I found an old lumpy couch in the church for Dad to stretch out on, and started making trips back and forth.

It seemed that the boxes of food and bags of clothes had multiplied during the trip. Only one other man, Ion Mehedinti, spoke any English. We started a conversation as we made trip after trip from the truck to the church warehouse. He was a tall, dark man with brown eyes and a steady smile. As we unloaded the truck, he explained some of the unique cultural beliefs that led to the country's sad shape.

"Though we lived under Communism for almost 50 years, the people clung to what Scripture they knew, or thought they knew," he explained. "One of the most damaging was the belief that women were literally saved through labor. Childbirth. They thought the more babies they had, the greater their chances of getting into heaven." This belief, coupled with the former dictator's desire to double the population, sure explained a lot.

I also learned that the layout of each of the tiny flats in the apartment-style building was identical: two rooms plus a tiny kitchen and bath. Parents typically stayed in one room, and the other room was used for as many children as they had. Everyone was crowded, hungry, and without hope that tomorrow would be any better than today.

> Communism's greatest enemy is family; they have spent generations educating the people here to depend on no one but the state, not God, not each other.

As we set down another load of boxes, Ion turned to me. "Have you ever heard of James Dobson?" It seemed like a weird question from a stranger here in the middle of nowhere.

"Yes, sure I have. He is one of the best-known teachers in America. I have never met him personally, but I love his work, his heart," I responded.

"I have heard just a few of his tapes," Ion continued. "Our people need practical teaching like that on family. Communism's greatest enemy is family; they have spent generations educating the people here to depend on no one but the state, not God, not each other. I need help to teach people God's way. I'd give anything for more of James Dobson's teaching."

Reaching into his pocket, he offered me a business card. I stuffed it in my jacket pocket as he finished. "When you get back, could you see if you could send me some tapes?"

I smiled tentatively, not wanting to say no, but not wanting to commit either. The last thing I needed was another obligation. I turned to get another load and noticed later that Ion was gone; I didn't see him again that trip.

A short while later, our truck was empty, and the warehouse was full floor to ceiling. The directions to the motel were in my hand, and I couldn't wait to get there. Slowly we made our way up the road. It was dark by now, and there were no streetlights. Everything looked ominous. Still, my mood was light and improving. We had delivered the goods, and I could head home having done well by my dad.

As we pulled into the motel, I tried to hide my reaction. Had this place been in any American inner city, I would have expected to see hookers and drug dealers in the corner of the parking lot. I paid for the room, took the key, and got my dad inside as quickly as I could.

When I flipped on the light switch by the door, a single flickering bulb cast a dim light in the room. The floor was a worn vinyl, some color of beige or gray. It had nothing extraneous, not even a trash can. The tattered orange and green bedspreads did little to conceal the bulges and lumps in the two beds, even in the dim light.

I cleaned up as best I could in the dingy bathroom and climbed into bed, tossing a "good night" to Dad as I turned off the light.

In no real hurry to be anywhere, we slept late the next morning. I wanted Dad to get as much rest as he could before the long trip back. He moved slowly, and as he removed his nightshirt, I could see the infection leaking from his bandage. Once home, surely he could sleep better and allow himself to rest and heal, knowing that the goods had been delivered to Romania.

After eating at a small café for breakfast, we decided to call on the pastor once more before we left. It was past noon when we returned to the church, and as we stepped out of the car, I saw the pastor running toward us from the building.

"I found it! I found it!" he shouted. With a big grin on his face, he continued, "You were right; there is an orphanage! It's right here, right down the street!"

He pointed to a gray flat, square building less than 1,000 yards from where we stood as he explained that it housed almost 200 babies and children. This was incredible! We'd be able to hand-deliver the goods ourselves, see the joy on the children's faces. I was ready to get busy, to move the food and supplies from the warehouse to the orphanage.

As I started toward the warehouse, though, the pastor grabbed my sleeve. He couldn't quite meet my eyes.

"I am sorry," he said, looking at his feet. "It's all gone."

It took a minute to sink in. Gone? "What do you mean, it's gone?" I asked.

"Everything. All the food. All the clothes, coats, medicine. The people here are starving. They have nothing. I didn't know the orphanage was here, and I couldn't just sit on things that could save lives. I did what I thought I should do. I am so sorry."

I didn't know whether to punch the guy or weep. Turning my back, I started to walk away, toward the orphanage. I couldn't look at him; I was afraid of what I might do or say. Instead, I focused on slowly putting one foot in front of the other.

At the door, my mind flashed to all the news stories I had seen, the video of the faces, and the rows of starving children with haunting eyes. Taking a deep breath, I tried to prepare for what awaited me on the other side.

> As it opened, the smell of human waste assaulted me in a way I had never experienced before.

In my hands, I held one lone box of formula that we'd somehow forgotten under the seat of the truck the day before—that was all I had. I had no money in my pocket beyond gas money to get home. There would be nothing on God's earth I could do for those babies that day, no matter what I found. Suddenly, I didn't want to go in. What would be the point?

I turned to my dad. "You go in if you want, but I am staying out here. I'll wait as long as you want. Take your time, and then we will go back home."

Dad looked up at me. His expression changed in an instant from that of a sick man to that of an angry, red-faced father of a rebellious child.

"You will go in there! You will go in there with me right now!" he demanded, stepping around me and swinging the door open.

As it opened, the smell of human waste assaulted me in a way I had never experienced before. It was dark inside, and I could hear metal cribs crashing into one another. The sounds of babies whimpering filled the room.

Ignoring Dad's demand, I turned my back on him and on the orphans and started back toward the truck.

"God, what on earth are You doing to me?" I muttered as much to myself as to God. "Let me go back home to my family. What am I doing here?"

I continued to walk away, calling over my shoulder, "No, Dad, I am not going in. I have nothing for them. And if I go in, if I see it and don't help, I am guilty. If I don't see it, it is someone else's problem. It's not mine."

He spun on his heels and came after me, grabbing me by the shoulders with strength I didn't know he had.

Between his teeth, he spat out, "You are already guilty. You know we have to help. You will not offend these people by not going in, and you will not disappoint the Lord and me. Now get in there."

I had no choice. My heart heavy, I walked slowly inside.

Tears started rolling down my cheek as soon as I stepped over the threshold. The smell of urine overwhelmed me. The hallway led from one massive room to the next, each filled with row after row of broken metal cribs with thin mattresses and chipped lead paint.

There were two infants in some, a single toddler in others. No child was properly clothed, especially given how cold it was. Some wore shirts; others wore nothing but tiny handkerchief-like cloths on their behinds. Their arms and legs looked like sticks, and their eyes were sunken deep into their faces.

They were covered in filth, human feces, urine, food they had thrown up. Each face was sadder than the last, surreal, beyond describing with mere words.

A few slept in spite of the horror and smell. A few stared off into nothingness, not making a sound, not moving a muscle, not noticing that I was there. Some of the toddlers stood holding onto the sides of their cribs, rocking with all their might. The rhythm of the crib rocking back and forth was all they had to soothe themselves.

There was not an adult to be seen in the room. These babies were alone in their misery, caged in their cribs, suffering from hunger and God knows what else.

And I had nothing to give them.

CHAPTER 3

HEART ATTACK!

WE DIDN'T LEAVE THAT day. Instead, we spent a few painful hours at the orphanage before heading back to the motel again, planning to go to bed early and start our trip home as rested as possible.

The next morning, Dad looked worse. He said little, his skin was ashen, and the spark in his eyes had gone. But that didn't stop me from barking at him to hurry along.

"I am leaving here in 30 minutes," I said as soon as my feet hit the floor. I'd gotten little sleep, and my emotions were riding a roller coaster of anger and sadness, helplessness, and—dare I admit it—shame. "If you aren't in the truck by then, I am leaving without you," I blurted out.

A few minutes later, Dad limped through the chill morning air toward the truck. It was starting to snow, and as soon as he climbed in, he closed his eyes. I was glad to see him nap—I was in no mood to chat. My whole world had been rattled from what I had seen and experienced at that orphanage.

So much had come at me so fast that I hadn't had time to digest it. As we started up the road, my mind wandered back in spite of my best efforts to think of anything else.

Were those really coffee cans that were being used to potty train the little ones? A row of cans lined the walls, the metal edges jagged, the tops cut off with some sort of crude can opener. Over time, the metal rusted, and the labels faded.

I had watched a lone worker take all of the children who were old enough to stand and force them to sit their naked little bums on these cans. She lined up 20 or more, and under her iron rule, the children would sit on those cans for hours at a time.

> How could she be so heartless?

My heart stopped each time a child rebelled for a moment and stood up. Deep cuts, the same shape and size as the tops of the cans, were swollen, raw, and oozing with infection across their tiny bums. Worse still, the monster of a woman in charge couldn't have cared less. She'd take them by the arms and violently force them back down on the cans, ignoring their pleas, their pain. How could she be so heartless?

Behind me, Dad let out a moan and shifted in his sleep. My thoughts turned to him. How was he handling what he saw? I'd never even given him a chance to really talk. As sick as he was, I knew his heart was aching for those babies more now than before he'd seen them himself.

All that work, all the calls, the favors, and for what? We hadn't helped the babies at all. I had wasted two weeks of my life, and no telling how much in airfare and lost income, and for what? To have the stuff taken from us without a bit of resistance. Disgusting, all of it.

Hours passed, and Dad still slept. Should I be worried? He'd slept all night and now most of the day, but maybe sleep was what he needed. The cassette player was off so it wouldn't disturb him, leaving nothing to invade my thoughts but what I had seen and smelled in Romania.

With no soap, the only way the workers could "clean" the make-shift diapers was by rinsing them out in cold water and hanging them over the radiators to dry. To minimize the number of diaper changes, the workers gave the babies as little water or formula as they could get away with. The few drops each child received several times a day was just enough to keep them alive, but never enough to satisfy them.

Not only were the children malnourished and dehydrated, but they were also in constant pain, too weak to cry on death's doorstep. Who cares?

"Really, who cares that these children are dying?" I said. My words, which I'd meant to keep to myself, caused Dad's eyes to flutter open.

"My Jesus cares," he said, and drifted back to sleep.

Two days, several shifts of drivers, and roadside stops blended together. We made good time, and as light was starting to break on the third morning, the signs announced that London was less than an hour away. Thankfully, we'd have time to get a real breakfast and still get to the other side of the city before heavy workday traffic slowed us down.

I noticed a truck stop and waved over the truck behind me. With any luck, it would be the last stop of the trip. Inside, tables of steaming eggs, toast, sausages, and bacon lined up before us. It was the first real meal we'd had since leaving Scotland.

Dad and the others settled into a back booth with their trays as I made my final selections. Just as I turned to follow them, I felt a stirring within me. I don't say this lightly, but the voice of the Lord spoke to me.

"Don't sit there with your dad. Sit on the other side, alone. Over there," I felt Him saying. Following His leading, I set my tray down, then went back to let my dad know I would not be joining him. I told him I was fine, not upset; I just needed a moment or two alone.

Across from where I had left my tray was a table of men, and I turned my back to ignore them. Just as I lifted my warm cup to my lips, I heard one of them utter the name of the Lord. With my emotions and nerves already on edge, I responded instantly, my head snapping around to face them. How dare someone use the name of my Lord and Savior in vain? I was going to give them a piece of my mind! But as I started to stand, I heard him complete his thought: Preach the gospel....

Now I was curious. We weren't exactly in a Communist country anymore, but someone speaking of the Lord in a public area like this was not something you heard often in the United Kingdom. I went over and introduced myself to the three men.

"Hi, my name is Philip Cameron," I said. "I am a preacher from Scotland, but I live in the United States now. I couldn't help but overhear you talk about the Lord."

They each shook my hand and smiled. As they introduced themselves, I learned that one was a top executive for James Dobson. James Dobson! It seemed surreal. I patted my jacket and found the business card from Ion still there.

"It's a long story," I explained, "but I am on my way back from Romania. The people there are hungry for teaching, especially about family, which is Dr. Dobson's specialty."

Handing him the card, I went on, "This man is a lay leader in his church, and he asked me specifically if I could send him some James Dobson teaching material when I got home. Could you help him?" He agreed to do what he could for a man who was a complete stranger to us both.

I finished my breakfast with a lighter heart. I had heard from God. He spoke to me, I listened, and a Christian brother in Romania would have his prayers answered.

It felt good—especially because I was not exactly proud of how I had responded to His call over the last few weeks. I had not treated my dad with the honor and respect he deserved. I had not responded with joy at the thought of making a difference on this trip, and I was still mad at God because all of our gifts had been taken. We had enough to change the lives of those babies. Why did God allow us to get so much and come so far just to have this happen? I didn't get it. I was angry, but I was relieved to know God still spoke to me...and I could hear Him!

Eight hours later, we arrived home. Mother greeted us before I could even get Dad's door open. Every bone in my body ached, screaming for a good night's sleep. I forgot to be polite, to help, to even unload my personal items from the car. I walked straight into the house and up the stairs and fell on the bed in my room. That is the last thing I remembered for 12 hours.

When I finally awoke, it was 6:00 in the morning. Outside the birds were chirping, but oddly that was the only sound I could hear. By this time, I would typically smell breakfast cooking or hear the teapot whistling. Had Mom overslept? I noticed that she had washed the clothes I'd been wearing the night before and had hung them on the back of the door. I wasn't worried, but I did think it was strange.

I took a shower and dressed in the clothes Mom washed. Taking my time, I made the bed and tossed the dirty clothes into my suitcase, thinking only about the flight schedules and what I needed to do before I could finally fly home.

"Mom?" I called as I walked down the steps. "Mom, are you there?"

Silence.

Knowing she'd be awake, I knocked on her bedroom door. She had had her quiet time at 5:00 every morning of my life.

"Mom?" Still no answer.

I opened the door to an empty room. Across the hall, the bathroom door was

> Your dad had a major heart attack.

open, but she wasn't in there either. In the kitchen, there was no sign of life. Where the heck was Mom? And where was Dad, for that matter? It was too early for them to be out and about, and it was totally unlike

Mom not to have started breakfast by now. A tiny dart of fear flew across my heart. Something was wrong, I could feel it. But what?

Walking out the door, I found my brother-in-law John getting out of a tiny blue car. "Where are Mom and Dad?" I asked before even saying hello.

"Philip, hi. I am sorry; don't you know? Your dad had a major heart attack. They tried to wake you, but they couldn't get a rise out of you. They couldn't wait any longer, so they rushed him to the hospital hours ago."

CHAPTER 4

A HERITAGE OF MIRACLES

HEART ATTACK?

This just didn't make sense. Closing my eyes for a split second, I tried to process what I'd just heard.

I should have known this was coming. After all, we had been side by side for almost 10 days, night and day! Sure, I knew that he was uncomfortable, but he was recovering from cancer surgery; of course he was uncomfortable. If he'd ever asked me to stop, to find a doctor or hospital, I would have.

Back inside, the house was eerily quiet without Mom and Dad. Suddenly, I felt like a little boy, abandoned, all alone. My dad was my rock; there was no one on earth I respected more. He was a part of me that went beyond father and son. Every sermon I had ever preached, every praise song I had ever written or sung, was because this man poured his life, his love of Jesus, his ministry, into me.

"Dear Lord," I prayed, "please don't let him die. It's too soon. I need him. My kids need him. This world needs him."

Knowing him as well as I did, it was hard to fathom that my father was not born into a household of believers. For the past 200 years, probably every male in his family had been a worthless alcoholic.

The stories about those bad boys were legendary. The Camerons were the town drunks. Everyone knew they would be first in line at the bar. If there was a fight, they started it. If there was someone in the gutter at the end of the night, it was a Cameron.

The name Cameron meant "worthless" in my hometown for generations. Dad's generation didn't start out any better. Dad's older brother Michael was a good-looking chap, shorter than Dad and stouter. He was a decade older than my father, and by the age of 18 he was a full-blown alcoholic.

My grandfather served in the military, and Michael was hired by the military as he came of age. His time in the service gave him nothing but money and freedom to develop his alcoholism further. Every weekend that he was on leave, he would travel by ferry to the mainland and head to a smoky bar.

> In that instant, the Holy Spirit convicted him, and he began to weep and shake as he read the Scriptures for the very first time.

He was no "life of the party" drunk. No, he would buy a bottle of rum, find a quiet place to sit in the corner, and drink until he passed out. When he came to, he'd drink some more until he passed out again. That was his life. As the weekend neared its end, he would somehow manage to drag himself back on a bus, nod off during the trip back to base, and muddle through the week until he could do it all again.

Even in his youth, the effects that the alcohol had on him were beginning to show. He felt terrible. His weight dropped, his skin looked yellow, and he had no will to live. His life revolved around the bottle, and there was no room for anyone or anything else.

But during one of these trips, something happened. One Monday morning, as he was waiting to catch a bus to a party, Michael realized he was hungry and had a little time. After walking into a quaint little tea shop, he settled at one of the tables by the window. After a quick look at the menu, he ordered a cup of tea and a sandwich.

While waiting for the waitress to return with his tea, something caught his eye. There, settled between the salt and pepper shakers, was a folded pamphlet. Mindlessly, he picked it up and began to read, "For God so loved the world, that He gave His only begotten Son...." (John 3:16, NASB).

In that instant, the Holy Spirit convicted him, and he began to weep and shake as he read the Scriptures for the very first time. Tears began to slide down his cheeks and onto the lace tablecloth. The waitress approached with his tea and immediately saw the tears.

Sinking into the chair beside him, the older lady looked into his eyes, took his hand, and asked, "Son, are you saved?"

He didn't know how to explain it, but he knew the Holy Spirit was working in him. He looked up and said, "Yes, I am; I'm saved!"

By the power of God, he was delivered instantly. He was released from the chains the demon of alcoholism had him in for so long.

The bus came and went, but he stayed to talk to the woman. "Where are these words from?" he asked, pointing to the pamphlet.

"They're from the Bible, son." The woman's kindness was evident in her words.

With John 3:16 fresh in his mind, my Uncle Michael met Jesus in that tea shop. The Cameron family has never been the same.

When he returned to base, he began knocking on every door during his off hours, saying, "I've met a man called Jesus, and He saved me. I found the words in this book, the Bible. Will you read it? You might find Him, too."

The very next weekend, he went to visit his relatives with a beat-up red suitcase full of Bibles and a silly grin on his face.

"We don't have to live like this," he announced to a less-than-enthusiastic gathering of his parents, aunts, uncles, and siblings—including my dad. Many of them stared at him from a haze of some stout drink.

"Really," he implored. "We don't have to be drunks!"

It wasn't a pleasant weekend for any of them, and he left feeling like he had made no progress and his family members were just happy to have him off their backs.

He returned to base at the end of his leave, disappointed by his family's reaction, but determined nonetheless. For seven years, he tried to reach his family for Jesus. For seven years, his whole family tried to talk him out of being a "religious fanatic."

> Again I prayed, pleading with God to save his life.

But nothing stopped Michael. His prayers, along with my mother's devotion years later, eventually led to Dad's belief in Christ. From the time he was saved, Dad had spent his entire adult life helping others, preaching, and sharing what God had done for him. He was a powerful force in the pulpit, a natural speaker, despite never being formally trained, and mentored more young preachers than anyone else I have ever met.

The thought of him on an operating table with his chest split open flashed in my mind. This just couldn't be happening to Dad!

Again I prayed, pleading with God to save his life. I was scared and hopping mad. How dare they not wake me when this happened? My dad had a heart attack, and they took him out of the house without even bothering to wake me! I could feel my blood beginning to boil. The conversation would not be pretty when I got to the hospital.

I had no idea if they had taken Mom's or Dad's car—or maybe even someone else's—and I didn't know where to start looking for a set of keys. Maybe on his dresser? No. Hanging by the kitchen door? No. I finally found a set in a candy dish on a hallway table.

Both car keys were on the ring, side by side. It figured. My parents were just like that. They really were a storybook couple.

I'd known from the time I was a little boy that I wanted a marriage like theirs. I wanted someone to look at me like that, someone who still made my heart flip decades after we wed. I wanted a best friend, someone who understood God's leading in my life and helped me follow those leadings. I found all that and more in my Chrissie. But without them as a model, I would never have known what to look for.

I'd heard their story a hundred times. They'd met at Uncle Michael's wedding in 1947. Mother had dressed with great care that night, as she always did. Her flame red hair was curled perfectly, and she wore a simple string of pearls to complement her light blue dress and black heels.

The band was playing a Perry Como tune that was just right for dancing, and my mom and her date were swaying to the music in the middle of the dance floor. As they danced, she put her head on his shoulder and scanned the room, mindlessly looking to see if any of her other friends had arrived.

It was then that she first saw my father, standing among others with his back against the wall. He was tall and thin, with thick wavy hair—a good-looking man who stood out in any crowd.

She tapped her date on the shoulder and pointed toward them.

"Who is that? I don't think I've ever seen them before," she asked innocently enough.

"Harrumph," her date snorted. "They are Camerons. They're not good people, no one you'd want to talk to. Hard to believe my cousin just married into that bunch." With that, he grabbed her waist a bit tighter and turned her away from them as the two of them danced.

His words and actions unnerved her. During the song, she stopped dead in her tracks in the middle of the dance floor. "Excuse me, but who do you think you are, telling me whom I should or should not talk to? I am not a child, and I do not belong to you!" she sputtered, her eyes flashing with rage.

To make her point, she made her way across the floor and soon was dancing with my Uncle John, and later with Dad. The music played on. Frank Sinatra. Nat King Cole. Romance was in the air. Before the night was over, she was quite taken with my father, and he with her.

For months they dated, fell in love, and were practically inseparable. Dad was just 16, and my mom was 18. Then, two unthinkable things happened: Dad received an official government mailing that announced he had been conscripted into the Army, and at the same time, my mother began to suspect that she was pregnant.

My father recalled my mother walking into Dr. Dingwall's office—the town family doctor—dressed as if she were about to be photographed for a fashion magazine, with her hair just so, wearing red high heels and a stunning formfitting dress.

Dad walked her to the front door and stayed outside to wait. To my father, the minutes seemed like hours as he stood watching, waiting. Then the front door opened. Mother stood straight and tall, trying to appear confident as she walked out the door. He was at her side in a few strides, and she wasted no time telling him the news.

"I am pregnant."

They walked in silence back to her house. When they arrived, she didn't even slow down, stepping inside and closing the door before Dad could say a word, much less follow her.

Helplessly feeling like his world had just exploded, my dad walked home. Scared and clueless about what to do next, he walked into his house and explained to his mother what had happened.

"I am going to marry her," he announced. "She is having my baby, and we need to get married right away."

"You will do no such thing, young man," his mother replied, turning on her heel and slamming the door behind her.

As my father told the story years later, he knew from the look on her face that this would not be discussed any longer. His mother was stern and set in her ways. She controlled the family with an iron fist. Dad knew there was no fighting her. He could not win, nor could he live without my mom. Heartbroken, he began to weep. He thought of the love of his life alone with a baby, his child, growing inside her, and the tears turned to wails of grief.

Heartbroken and desperate, my father locked himself in the tiny bathroom. He wanted to die, for the pain to stop. He grabbed a bottle of pills and swallowed a fistful of aspirin. When his parents finally got the bathroom door open, he was vomiting all over the floor.

As the waves of nausea settled down hours later, he looked up from his seat on the bathroom floor to a sight he had never seen in his 16 years: his mother crying.

His father put his arms around him and rocked him back and forth like he was cradling a child. "Don't do this, son," he pleaded. "We love you. You are a man now, and if you love this girl, of course you can marry her."

Seven months later, in 1948, the young married couple was living behind my grandparents' house in a tiny six-by-ten-foot room with no running water and a single cord that brought electricity from the main house, awaiting both the birth of their baby and the date that my dad would have to report for military duty.

The child, whom my parents named Simon after his father (a Scottish tradition), was a lovely boy with a tuft of reddish hair, bright blue eyes, and a round, red face. He cried loudly, ate heavily, and slept in two-hour shifts. Three days after his birth, the tiny baby stopped breathing. Immediately my mother leaped to her feet and wailed, "Simon, quick, something is wrong with the baby!"

> Finally, all he could do was go home and accept that his baby was gone.

After taking a quick look at the baby's still face, my father ran out the door and down the street. Stealing a bike along the way, he rushed to the nearest doctor's office and burst through the doors without knocking.

"Get out!" the doctor barked.

"You don't understand. My baby is dying," my dad begged.

"If your baby is dying, he will be dead before I get there," the doctor snapped coldly, turning his back on my father. "Now get out!"

Dad closed the door behind him and began weeping loudly and uncontrollably, still standing on the front step, longing to hear the doctor open the door and offer to save his baby. Sorrow turned to anger. Anger to despair. Finally, all he could do was go home and accept that his baby was gone.

Adding to the heartache, just days later on a misty gray morning, my mother watched my father board a train to boot camp. They said nothing as they stood on the platform until the final call. Each carried a pain too great to even speak. She kissed him good-bye and walked the long way back to their broken-down shack—a place that felt as empty as her heart.

While my father was away in the service, my mother busied herself with work. Among her many jobs, she took a job as a maid. During that time, two men came to town to hold a revival meeting. Their names were Donald Walker and Herbert Harrison, and they slept in a converted meat truck, making their beds on the cold metal that had once held slabs of meat. Each night, they held a revival meeting, which started a buzz across town. The Holy Spirit was moving.

Out of sheer curiosity, my mother attended a few of their services.

By the time they left town, seven years after Michael started praying, 96 people had been saved. Two thirds of them were Camerons, including my mom.

My mother found her way to the altar when she heard the words of Matthew 16:26: "What good will it be for someone to gain the whole world, yet forfeit their soul? Or what can anyone give in exchange for their soul?" (NIV).

Jesus provided a safe harbor for this brokenhearted young woman who lost her first child and was separated from her husband so early in their marriage. Church became her whole life while my dad was serving around the world. Working through her grief and loneliness, she dug into the Word of God and attended every service and Bible study she could.

Although Dad sent his paycheck home every week, my mother struggled to get by. The Army paid him a single man's wages because there was no pay scale for a married man his age.

My mother and father wrote to each other often while he was deployed. Mom's letters were devoted to sharing her new faith; Dad's letters were sent with harsh commands to "get out of that religion." But my mother would counter his demands, saying she could not become "unborn."

By the time he came home in September 1951, both of my parents were very different people—strangers living under the same roof. Mom had grown closer to God each day and faithfully tithed from Dad's tiny paycheck, while my father had become an angry drunk with an eye for women. He'd order her to go with him to bars and drinking parties, and he beat her terribly if she refused. My mother was too afraid to tithe or to even attend church, fearing what he might do if he found out she was "spending money on the church."

One Saturday afternoon, she went into town with my father to pick up a few things. While he wandered off in one direction, my mother ran into some ladies from the church. They chatted a bit, catching up, and she tried to evade their questions about her attendance at church. Just as Dad came up behind her, she blurted: "I feel so guilty. I have not paid my tithes since Simon got home. We are still living in a shack behind his parents' house. I cook on a camp stove. We sleep in a twin bed. We only have two plates, two bowls, two cups, two forks, and a few clothes. And we have a baby on the way! He would never understand."

"Understand what?" he barked from behind her. "What is a tithe, anyway?"

Mother explained to him that the Bible teaches that we are to give ten percent of our earnings to the Lord each week, bracing for the outburst that was sure to follow.

"So you're supposed to give God 10 percent, and you have been giving nothing? You go back there and start giving 15 percent until you make up every last penny. I can't afford to have God mad at me!" he blurted. He spun on his heel and headed back toward the house, Mother following a few steps behind.

> She knew God was working on Dad.

With that, my mother started tithing 15 percent until she was "caught up." She knew God was working on Dad. From that point on, every now and then, he would go to church with her. The preachers knew exactly the kind of life he was living and would turn up the flames of hell with their words as they preached. Dad simply sneered back at them.

Mother endured a lot in the seven years before Dad was saved. Many good Christian women would have walked out. Instead, she stayed and prayed. In 1952, she gave him a daughter, Wendy, and then she gave him me three years later.

I didn't come into the world easily. When Mom's contractions began, I was breech, racking her thin body with pain. Dr. Dingwall came to the house and stayed for days, fearful of losing us both. With nothing to ease her pain, he had to reach inside my mother and turn me around. All this was done in that tiny, crude shack in which they lived. For 48 hours, this kind doctor stayed with my mother, sang to her, and comforted her, until he felt we were stable enough to be on our own.

Mother was so grateful for his care. Months later, when I was still an infant, she started helping the doctor and his wife in their home—the same house she had often admired as a child.

Both Dr. Dingwall and his wife struggled with alcohol abuse, but it didn't deter my mother. She would help them out of bed, toss out the empty bottles of booze, and prepare his office so that he could attend to patients.

Out of appreciation for what he had done for her, she also cleaned, cooked, and ran errands—anything she could do to serve him. My mother would care for the doctor and his wife in the mornings, and my father would spend the evenings drinking. My sister, Wendy, often would hear my mother crying while he was out.

"Lord, keep him safe tonight," Mother would pray through her tears.

She continued to pray, saying, "Give me grace, God. Give me the grace to live with him one more hour, one more day, one more year." She never knew what would set him off.

One afternoon, he stomped into their shack for his lunch, and my mother knew she was in trouble before he even opened his mouth.

"I hate you, and I hate God," he roared. "I am finished with you!" With that, he stormed out and went back to his work cutting wood.

That afternoon, the electric saw screamed as he cut one piece of wood after the other, sawdust flying everywhere. He paused a moment to wipe his brow and check his watch. It was almost 4:00 p.m.

As he picked up another piece of wood to feed into the saw, the Holy Spirit began speaking to his heart. He'd never encountered or experienced anything like it. He began to sob. Shaking and weeping, he continued to feed wood into the saw, his voice rising over the noise so loudly that his brother John rushed over to see what was wrong.

"Simon, Simon, what's the matter with you, boy? Are you hurt? What is wrong?"

Shaking his head, all my dad could say was, "I don't know."

"Well, get off that saw before you cut your arm off!" John said as he led him away to the shop office. After helping him onto the battered old sofa, John got him some tea and ordered him to stay there while he fetched my mother.

In mere minutes she was there, trying to determine what was wrong with her husband—the man who, just hours before, had announced he was leaving her.

"Tell me what happened," she said.

John shook his head and told her how Simon had just started sobbing, right out of the blue. "And he kept saying the strangest thing: 'I'm not worthy. I'm not worthy,'" he explained, a bewildered look on his face.

Mother walked over to the sofa and put her small hand on my father's tear-stained face. "I know what is wrong with you, Simon Cameron. The Holy Ghost has got a hold on you. The Bible says that if you call on the name of the Lord, you will be saved."

Dad's cry instantly transformed from a sob to a shout, "Jesus, take me!" And with that, he was born again. My father was 25 years old and had been married for nine years, and suddenly, he had a new life.

I don't remember anything of my dad's past life. I was only two years old when he was saved; I have never smelled alcohol on his breath, never heard the Lord's name taken in vain, never seen him act like anything but what he was: a married Christian man who loved God and lived his life for Him.

He was a legacy. He really was. Now he was in some dreary hospital, clinging to life. And I had to get there. Fast.

CHAPTER 5

THIS IS YOUR SON

WHEN I ARRIVED AT the hospital, Dad was sleeping in a bed at the far end of the ICU.

The stark white sheets made him look paler, thinner, and frailer than I had ever seen him. My heart caught in my throat as I looked at him, guilt washing over me like a wave. I wanted to cry, to scream. I wanted him to forgive me for taking so long to get to Scotland, for allowing him to go to Romania on that giant goose chase, for sleeping through his heart attack. Instead, I stood silently by his bed and prayed.

> A pitiful little cough escaped him, and then he repeated what he had said: "There are babies dying."

Tubes and wires attached him to the various machines behind him that bleeped as they danced to their own tune. Nurses hurried by without a word. A few beds down someone called a Code Blue, and suddenly, the room was filled with all manner of medical professionals frantically working on the patient. In spite of their efforts, the woman died.

Her passing touched me deeply, underscoring how fragile life is, especially in the ICU. How could my dad, Simon Cameron, be lying in a hospital bed so close to death?

I closed my eyes and prayed, "Dear Jesus, please heal my dad. Touch him as only You can. I love him so much, Father. I need him. We all need him. Heal him...."

A noise from his bed startled me. Dad was waking up, and the tube down his throat was bothering him. He gurgled what seemed to be a few words. I moved closer and asked him to repeat himself.

A pitiful little cough escaped him, and then he repeated what he had said: "There are babies dying."

It was a moment of complete clarity. I suddenly knew exactly what I needed to do, what the Lord was saying to me, what would allow Dad to settle back, relax, and recover.

With my hand on his shoulder, I said, "Dad, I know there are babies dying. I saw them, too. They are mine now. As soon as you are a little bit better, I promise I will get on a plane, go back to America, and raise the money we need to really make a difference for those orphans.

They were mine now.

"They need more than a truck of food and diapers. It's going to take a lot of money, but I have lots of friends in ministries and churches, and I am going to get every last one of them involved. We'll help those babies."

Before I could get all of the words out, he was asleep again. I had no idea how much he'd heard, but it didn't matter. I made a vow to him, to the Lord, and to those Romanian babies. They were mine now.

I pulled up a chair and watched him sleep for a while, praying, thinking, planning my next moves. Suddenly, nothing on my calendar seemed appealing or exciting.

I didn't want to go on Christian television and sing happy praise songs. I didn't want to preach the salvation message to an audience surrounded by other preachers, churches, and programs that detailed the Roman Road to Salvation every 20 minutes. Americans literally had the gospel at their fingertips; just one click of the remote, and another preacher on television would deliver the message.

All I could think about was those babies. I felt like a man who knew there was a building on fire with children inside. I had to hurry. Mind you, I had no idea how to do that, what it would cost, what governmental red tape might be involved, how I would overcome the language barrier. But my course was set. Every lost moment meant more lost lives. I had to rescue as many babies as the Lord allowed.

Two weeks later, Dad was doing better, and I was in America. I slept little, working around the clock calling every person I had ever met and asking for help for the children of Romania. I flew all over the country, zigzagging from the East Coast to the West, telling the story of what I had seen in any church that would have me. I had no photos, no videos, no handouts of what I had seen; all I had was my firsthand story, my passion, and the anointing of God.

But that was enough. The money came from all over, and I was back on that 22-hour truck ride from Scotland to Romania with enough money and supplies to begin changing the lives of the babies I'd met.

With Dad still recovering, I took several of my dad's former students with me, including Brian Paterson, who was now working for the ministry. We started at the orphanage we found on our first trip, supplying it with food, diapers, potty-chairs, and more. We replaced the old wooden window frames so that the place would be warm through the harsh winter months. I worked with local contractors, supervising the jobs to make sure every dollar was spent properly, and watched as lives were being changed.

I was pouring cash into buildings that were owned by a Communist country, but I would not let that deter me. That wasn't the point. The point was that babies were dying of starvation and neglect.

Over the next few months we made several trips, and once things were well underway, we brought Christmas boxes and candies. The children's faces changed as their health improved. We were met with bright smiles and giggles on every trip back to Romania. We were delighted to see the children gaining weight, to see the color returning to their skin.

On one trip, after seeing radical improvement at the first home, we set out to find another Romanian orphanage before returning to the United States.

It had snowed all night, and the day was gray and bitterly cold. The wind blew the snow across the potholed road as we navigated slowly toward a home. We had been told that it was "really bad," but after what we had seen, how bad could it be?

The snow was falling hard, and the large, fluffy flakes made it difficult to see. When we finally arrived, I tried to open the door of the truck. It was frozen shut. I slammed my shoulder into the metal door with all my might, and with a creak it finally opened. My loafers were soaked the instant I stepped out into the snow. For a moment, I wished that for once in my life I'd worn boots.

> I'd be back again...and again.

Carefully, I stepped through the angry blizzard. I opened the gate and let myself into the yard. I had started toward the building but then stopped dead in my tracks. What was I seeing? Through the snow, I could see something—someone—outside in the yard.

"No," I told myself, "there can't be anyone sitting out in this storm, but...."

It was a girl, no more than five years old, sitting there all alone. As I drew closer, she looked in my direction without focus, and I could immediately tell that she had Down syndrome.

"Hi, sweetheart," I said softly as I walked toward her.

Someone—some monster—had left her tied to the old rusty chair in which she was sitting. Back and forth she rocked herself, mumbling words I could not understand. She was wearing only a thin jacket, and despite the bitter cold, she had nothing on her feet but socks with holes in them. It took a few minutes to untie her. When I was finally able to release her, she clung to me like a drowning person to a life raft.

I took her inside and found worse conditions than I had ever seen—these were babies on whom the people of Romania had given up. Many of the children were physically deformed, while others were mentally challenged. As I walked the halls, I found still others who were critically ill and dying.

No one cared. This was a warehouse for these babies; that's all it was. If there had ever been any doubt in my mind that this would be the driving passion of my life, it was settled in that moment. I'd be back again...and again.

Each trip was a whirlwind of hiring contractors, delivering goods, and getting to know each of the children. It was a long and slow process, but finally, I felt at peace, knowing that the children I had come to love finally would have a warm home.

Finally, Dad was healthy enough to travel with me to Romania. I couldn't wait for him to see all that we had accomplished since our initial trip. He would hardly recognize the first place, or the children he'd met; I couldn't wait to show him.

We spent a happy afternoon delivering more goods, playing with the children, enjoying the happy sounds they made. Gone was the nasty smell that had hung in the air on our first visit. Gone was the look of hopelessness on the children's faces. Even the workers seemed happier and more engaged. They had food to feed their charges, diapers, and laundry detergent—the simple things that make all the difference.

"This is your son."

I also showed Dad the other homes we were helping, stopping in each one long enough to visit all the children.

We walked into one upstairs room, and there, three rows back, was a little boy sucking in his cheeks. As the other children rocked back and forth in their cribs, he stood still, watching me. Locking eyes with him, I started walking toward his crib, talking to him in a singsong voice. As I neared the crib, I heard a voice as clear as a bell.

"This is your son."

I was dumbstruck. I knew as well as I knew my name that I had just heard the voice of the Lord. Like Moses before the burning bush, I knew God was there; He had spoken. My life was changing.

To ground myself, I needed to let Dad know what had happened.

"Dad," I said, reaching for his elbow, "Dad, look at that boy. Look at that face." Stopping, he turned with me.

Piercing green eyes stared back at us.

"Aye," said Dad as he nodded and turned his attention to a child in another bed. "He is a bonny boy."

Forcefully, I said, "No, Dad." The tone of my voice caught his attention more than the words I said. He looked at me carefully.

My voice softened, and I swallowed hard, "God wants me to adopt this boy."

I walked over and reached for the child, who looked to be no more than two years old. He was thin as a rail, and though his eyes were alert, he could barely speak a word of Romanian, and certainly could not speak English. I was astonished to learn later that he was four years old.

He practically leaped into my arms. It didn't matter that he had nothing on but a tattered old shirt or that his hair was matted to his head. It was evident the boy had not been washed in weeks; the smell was overwhelming. None of it mattered. I held him and rocked him, knowing that this was my son.

My son. God was giving me this boy.

I held him close, soothing him, falling in love with him.

Softly I spoke into his ear, "I don't know who you are or how you got here, but I promise, I will make you my son."

CHAPTER 6

AGAINST ALL ODDS

THE TRIP HOME WAS a blur—there's not much about it that I can remember. What I do remember is being so emotionally bonded to this child that I felt physically attached to him. I knew God intended for him to be mine. Every step I took away from him, every minute on an airplane, every mile I drove toward home, took me farther away from my boy, and it was physically painful.

When I pulled into the driveway of my lovely home, I sat in the car for a moment. Just the sight of the house was usually enough to lift my spirits, especially after a long trip. That home held everything I loved most.

Everything...until now.

I was attached to that little boy in Romania, as if an invisible umbilical cord led from the darkest heart of that country to mine as I sat outside my sunny home.

I didn't want my family to see my face and know that I was a mess inside. Trying to gather my nerve, I opened the car door. I was aware with every breath that my announcement would change the lives in our family forever. Bringing home this baby I had fallen in love with would demand a sacrifice. No one would feel it more than my wife, but my children also would be affected.

After a few moments, I slid out of the car. Stretching my legs, I looked around the yard. Two bicycles, bright and shiny, leaned against the garage. A soccer ball, still so new that there were no scuff marks on it, rested in the high grass by the fence, and the bright yellow slide on the swing set sat invitingly in the backyard.

His name was Andrew. He was miles away in a rusty crib, rocking back and forth, back and forth, with no one, nothing. The contrast was staggering.

Blinking back a tear, I lifted my suitcase out of the car and walked quickly to the door.

> "How would you feel about having another baby?"

Chrissie was standing with her back to me at the kitchen sink, washing the supper dishes, when I arrived. Hearing me come in, she turned and smiled at me over her shoulder. Without a word, I dropped my suitcase at the door and wrapped my arms around her waist, drinking in the magic of holding her in my arms again.

She leaned into my embrace and turned to hug me.

"I am so glad you are home," she said, and started to tell me about some school event that Philip Jr. had planned that night.

I tried to listen, to be polite, but I just couldn't. I was still holding her there at the sink, and she was still chattering, but I heard none of it. Finally, I interrupted, just blurted it right out there: "How would you feel about having another baby?"

That left my dear wife speechless. That question might not have sounded all that strange for a young man to ask his wife. But coming from me, it was.

Few things in life was I more convinced of than that no one should have more than two children. Chrissie had heard me lecture for hours upon hours to anyone willing to listen. I had blessed anyone I shared a holiday meal, an airplane row—even some church gatherings—with, with my flawless, well-crafted argument.

It started like this: How could any couple possibly give enough love and attention to more than two? Then I would detail the costs: education, weddings, minivans instead of cars, larger houses, and more food and utilities. Looking back, I made a real pest of myself repeating my "logic" to my siblings (not that they listened; my sisters, Wendy and Louise, each have three children).

Chrissie and I already had two. Until this moment, we were done. This story was written, and no one knew it better than Chrissie. She stepped back and looked up at me with her dear face, her eyes searching mine. Had I gone mad? Was this a joke? Or perhaps simply an opening line for a night of romance?

> Life changed that day, from that very moment.

Words failed me. I didn't know how to begin explaining what had happened, how I could possibly be asking her about another baby. Silently, I reached in my pocket and pulled out the small black and white photo that I had gotten developed on my way home.

"Andrew," I announced.

Chrissie didn't say a word. After drying her hands on her jeans, she took the photo out of my hand and stared at it, then looked back into my eyes, still searching for an explanation.

I didn't know how to verbalize what had happened. She looked down again at the little face staring back at her from the photo.

"Oh, yes," she said.

And that was that. A quiet peace fell over the room. She continued to look at the photo, holding it as carefully as she held her own children—too precious to hold, too dear to let go.

After a moment, she broke the silence. "How soon can I meet him?"

Life changed that day, from that very moment. We both became singly focused. The more I shared about our boy, the more restless and determined we both became. The Bible says you have not because you ask not. I started asking.

First, I called every name I had listed in my Rolodex—pastors and businessmen all around the country. Many of them had been friends of my dad's for decades; others were new friends whom I had ministered to in their churches, whose lost loved ones I had prayed for, or whom I had met in ministry somewhere along the way.

From that moment on, every conversation revolved around Andrew.

"It's 7:00 in the morning there now; he'll just be waking up. Oh, I pray they have some cereal to give him....I got a call from Pastor So-and-So with $1,000; we only need $800 more to buy two plane tickets to go see Andrew...."

We prayed for him like nothing before. We prayed as a couple. We prayed as a family. The children were excited at the thought of having a little brother. While we didn't want to get their hopes up, we wanted them to be praying, for them to be part of the miracle. I prayed from the time I woke up until my last thought crossed my mind and I fell into sleep at night.

Andrew. My son. Our son.

"Lord, keep him safe until we can claim him as our own. Let no harm come to him," I prayed all night and day.

Every day was agony. We had no control or information about what was happening to him. He was only ours in our hearts, but he had filled our hearts so much; he was part of our every breath.

The days turned to weeks; the weeks, to months. Only seeing the steady flow of money coming in kept me sane. I knew God was in control. I knew He had perfect timing. But it was maddening!

One of my trips for the ministry took me to Greenville, South Carolina, to a ministry run by Jimmy and Joanne Thompson. They were an amazing couple and force of God, two people God chose out of very ordinary beginnings to do extraordinary things for the kingdom.

What had started as a small church was now an outreach that included a publishing/printing firm and a 24-hour Christian television network.

They shared my passion for orphans, especially those in Romania. When I was a guest there, I met a woman who pressed a folded piece of paper into my hand.

"Contact my friend Daniela when you get back to Romania," she said. "She helped a friend of mine from Canada adopt. She knows all the ropes and will gladly help you."

Thanking her, I tucked the paper safely into my wallet. The Lord knew I needed all the help I could get.

CHAPTER 7

THE JOURNEY
FOR ANDREW

MONTHS LATER, WE FINALLY had enough money to start our journey back to Andrew. Chrissie talked like a nervous school-girl on the flight over, fretting about the bed she set up for him at home and the new toys she had in her luggage. But once the plane landed, she grew quiet.

I knew my girl well enough to know she was in deep conversation with the Lord. Part of her was worried, unsure of the challenges we might face; part of her was filled with silly fears that Andrew might not like her.

After a restless flight to Vienna and more than six hours of driving across three countries, Chrissie and I slowly pulled into the parking lot of a small motel in Arad, Romania.

Before leaving Alabama, we'd been able to contact the woman whose name had been given to us—Daniela—to see what help she could give us. She was very pleasant on the phone and readily agreed to travel with us to find Andrew's birth mother and help us make the boy our own.

As we pulled into the motel parking lot, I saw a woman standing off to the side of the building where we had planned to meet. She was our only connection, and I had faith that she would be a great help.

Though I was happy to see her, her appearance startled me. I'm not sure what I expected, but she was perhaps 30, with a cold, harsh look about her. She was wearing skintight jeans—uncommon behind the previous Iron Curtain—and wore her long brown hair pulled back in a severe ponytail, with huge gold hoops hanging from her ears.

I had no reason to judge her on her appearance alone, but a flood of disappointment washed over me. It was scary to admit to myself how much hope I was pinning on this rough-looking woman. But at that point, I had no other choice. She was the only plan I had.

We exchanged hellos. After checking in to the motel, we mapped out our game plan for the next day. She sounded knowledgeable and bright. Pushing my fear aside, we set a time to meet her in the morning and wished her a good night.

After a fitful night of sleep, I awoke the next morning totally disoriented. My stomach grumbled impatiently as I momentarily waited for Chrissie to bring me my breakfast, as she did every morning. What would she make today? Perhaps poached eggs? Maybe a slab or two of ham? Or better yet, a steaming stack of pancakes?

> Unless we were successful in adopting him—and quickly—we would lose him forever.

But as I opened my eyes and the small, dreary motel room came into focus, I finally realized where I was and what I was doing there. Andrew's face came flooding back to me, my thoughts of breakfast forgotten immediately.

From the bathroom, I could hear Chrissie's voice in the shower. I couldn't tell if she was praying, singing, or talking to herself. But I knew from her tone that with every breath she took, she was becoming more determined and more ready for the battles ahead.

I wished I felt the same way. The challenges of adopting this child were going to be great. Unless we were successful in adopting him— and quickly—we would lose him forever. We couldn't let that happen. As I sat on the edge of the lumpy gray bed, I began to pray, my soul crying out at the thought of the boy staying even one more day where he was now.

Soon after, I felt the Holy Spirit begin to stir. My prayer of sadness became a prayer of hope, a hope so strong that it made no sense at all in the flesh. With my hands clasped together, I began to pray for the people we would meet along our path that day and in the days to come.

I prayed for those people who could help us, those people whose names I didn't know, those people we needed to share our goal: making this boy our own. I didn't know the names or even the titles of the government workers whose grace and assistance we needed, but God did.

I prayed for Andrew's mother, that she would see the love we had for her son, that she would allow us to become his family. I prayed for the woman with the paperwork at the orphanage, that her heart would be moved, that she would be given the wisdom to help and a passion to see this done. I prayed for the woman changing Andrew's diapers, for kindness, an extra measure of care. I prayed for Daniela, that she would be able to help us. I prayed that God would help us show this boy love, real love, starting today.

My wife came out of the shower, smiling at me in a way that melted my heart, her blonde hair hidden under the threadbare towel. She was my partner in all things. I never felt stronger than when she was by my side. She was the greatest gift God had ever given me in this world.

"Let's go get our boy," she said without a hint of doubt or fear.

I suddenly felt a sense of urgency and headed for the shower. It was time. God was moving in my heart, and I knew He was moving in others', too.

Soon after, with Daniela directing us, we settled in for the ride to the city where both Andrew and his birth mother would be found. We were quickly through a half dozen roundabouts and out of the city. The full sun was bright in the sky. Though the roads were rough, we rode in comfortable silence.

A dull, low scream behind me interrupted the quiet, and I instinctively hit the brakes and turned my head toward the sound.

"Daniela!" I shouted, quickly pulling off to the side of the road. "What on earth? Are you okay? What is wrong?"

Her eyes were closed, her arms wrapped around her waist, and still she moaned. Finally, she spoke. "I am pregnant," she admitted. "It is just cramps. Bad ones. Next week I am going to have an abortion. I'll be fine. Keep driving."

An abortion? This woman who I was told was helping rescue babies—like my Andrew—was planning to kill her own? Who was this woman in my car? What was I supposed to do now?

Her pains continued, and I couldn't ignore her screams.

I quickly found a gas station, and Chrissie led Daniela to the bathroom, half carrying her across the parking lot. Soon after, 10 minutes had passed. Then 20. Forty-five minutes had passed when the women finally returned, and I got back in the car.

When I saw that she had stretched across the backseat and appeared to be napping, I increased the speed and tried not to think about how much hope we had pinned on her.

An hour later, we arrived at the university that Dana, Andrew's birth mother, attended. Daniela had pulled herself together. Leaving us in the car, she went to find Dana.

The wait for her return was unbearable. I wanted to cry; I wanted to laugh; I wanted to pee; I wanted to do everything all at once. My nerves were so raw. I was about to meet a stranger who held the power to grant me the greatest desire of my heart—Andrew—or tear him away from us forever. She alone would validate what I had heard from God, that he was my son.

Finally, we saw Daniela and Dana crossing the parking lot. When they reached the car, Dana immediately burst into tears. She couldn't look at me. The flood of emotions rattled me, but I pressed on.

After introducing myself, I turned to Chrissie. "Hi, I'm Philip," I stammered. "This is my wife, Chrissie, and we love your son."

Before I said another word, she asked us to take her to meet her boyfriend, Vio. It was clear that she could not face this conversation alone.

We found Vio across town as he was coming out of the sports complex where he played on the Romanian handball team. Dana jumped out of the car and ran to him, and I could tell that she was describing us without really knowing who we are or what she was supposed to do. Eventually, he joined us in the car.

Back at Dana's dorm, we all got to know one another. We learned that while Vio wasn't Andrew's biological father, he loved Dana and the child very much, and he was fiercely protective of them; I could tell he wasn't too keen on us.

I asked Dana to share what had happened, how her child had come to live in an orphanage. Her story was one of the saddest I had ever heard. As she spoke, tears poured down her cheeks.

Dana, a short young lady with dark hair and sad eyes, was only a teen when she fell hard for a good-looking, fast-talking young man whom she met at the university. Their courtship had developed from stolen kisses to dreams of the future.

But when Dana found out she was pregnant, everything turned sour. He did not want a baby; he was not ready for responsibility. He held her hand, looked into her eyes, and promised to help "take care of the problem." She would have an abortion. It was not up for discussion; it was a directive. He knew of a clinic on the other side of town; all they needed to do was get their hands on some money before her pregnancy moved into the second trimester, when an abortion would cost more.

Neither was working, so they had very little money to get by. Finally, Dana had an idea. She had one piece of jewelry that was precious to her. With tears in her eyes, she handed her delicate gold bracelet to her boyfriend to sell for the money they needed. He took it from her hand, kissed her on the cheek, and promised to call the next day to make the necessary plans and appointments.

It was the last she ever heard from him. Friends said he sold the bracelet and headed straight for the sunny beaches on the other side of the country.

Dana was all alone. Fear ruled her life. She was scared her mother would discover her pregnancy and take her out of the university. She ate little, slept little, and silently begged a god she didn't know for it all just to go away.

It was an unusually warm fall day when she went into labor on September 21st. With no other options, she walked two miles to the nearest hospital. Alone. There, she was turned away because she had no money.

"You have to go to the hospital for the poor," she was told.

Alone again, she walked across town while her labor progressed, resting at bus stops and park benches with each contraction. She was in the middle of a bustling city, in midday, but either no one noticed her pain, or no one cared.

She walked for another three miles before she finally saw the hospital in the distance. The sun was going down. Sweat poured off her swollen body. Her shoes were stained and wet from when her water had broken. She had eaten nothing in more than 24 hours, and the contractions were then less than a minute apart.

To her horror, she was told, "I am sorry, ma'am. We are full. Every bed is taken." Dana met the woman's words with a loud groan, doubling over in front of her desk.

"Help me," Dana gasped through her clenched teeth. "Please. My baby is coming...."

As workers scrambled to get her into a wheelchair and down the crowded hall to the delivery room, Dana collapsed. Almost as soon as they had her undressed, the baby's head crowned. A nurse cursed, her planned lunch suddenly canceled.

Silently, the doctor and his team went about their work. Not one word of comfort or encouragement was wasted on this poor young woman.

Andrew was born and let out a thin murmur instead of a lofty cry. Pulling off his gloves with a snap, the doctor headed for the door, with one of the nurses following behind with Andrew in her arms.

Dana was left all alone.

Twenty minutes later, an orderly came to remove her from the delivery room, just as she was starting to doze off. She was taken to a small dirty room at the end of the hallway.

There, Dana was forced to share not just a room, but also a bed with another patient. Her bedmate was a gypsy, a class of society that was deeply despised in Romania. But what choice did she have? Dana bit back any protest she had, passed out from exhaustion, and slept for most of the next day.

Dana woke up cramped, hungry, and scared. The hospital did not provide food for its patients, and there was no one to bring Dana anything to eat. When the gypsy woman had her fill of what little food her family brought her, she, in her kindness, shared it with Dana.

Hours passed. Dana knew that the hospital would not keep her much longer, and she had nowhere to go. She thought about her options. There were no close friends or extended family members who would take in her and the baby. She didn't even have a dollar to her name.

And then there was her mother. Strict, judgmental, ruling their house with an iron fist. There was no way her mother would open her home to the baby; Dana would be lucky if her mother even took her back!

Soon, her exhaustion overcame her racing mind, and Dana drifted off to sleep. When she awoke again, a nurse with a clipboard was standing at her bedside.

"What time will your ride be picking you and the baby up?" she asked. "The latest you can stay is 2:00 p.m."

Dana glanced at the clock on the far wall. It was already 10:00 in the morning.

After waiting as long as she could, she called her mom and told her the truth through fits of tears, begging for her help. In no time, Dana's mother arrived with an empty paper bag and a grim look on her face. She never asked to see the baby, never asked about her daughter's healing, just quickly found her way around the room, loaded Dana's clothes and shoes into the bag, and headed for the door.

> Before she left she announced, "When you are ready to sign that baby over to the state, I'll give you back your clothes."

Before she left, she announced, "When you are ready to sign that baby over to the state, I'll give you back your clothes."

By then, it was already 1:00 in the afternoon. Dana had nothing to wear but the soiled hospital gown she had on, not even a pair of socks. She had one hour to make a decision that would affect her and her baby for the rest of their lives.

Andrew became a ward of the bankrupt country of Romania, a so-called "economic orphan," with parents alive but unable to care for him. He was one of thousands and thousands of hopeless orphans.

When Dana stopped telling her story, I cleared my throat and started to ask the most difficult question I have ever asked. How does one even begin to ask a mother to give her child away forever to total strangers who live half a world away?

"Dana," I said softly, "your story breaks my heart. I know you love your baby more than life itself."

Dropping her head to her chest, Dana stared down at the floor, refusing to look in my direction.

"Chrissie and I love him, too. I know it sounds crazy, but we love him like he is our own. Ever since I met him a few months ago, he is all I think about, pray about. I want to give him a life, a real future.

"We live in America. We have two children who would love to have him as their little brother. He'll never be without. We will raise him to know the Lord, give him a good education, and love him with all our hearts. Would you consider allowing us to adopt your son?"

The room grew quiet; only the faint sounds of traffic outside evaded the silence. I started to say more, but I stopped myself. A few moments passed, and I realized I was holding my breath. A prayer escaped my heart, "Please, Lord, don't let her ask for any money."

Even as tightly as my heart was wrapped around this boy, I knew that it was vitally important that one day, as this boy's father, I would be able to look him in those green eyes and tell him without a shadow of a doubt that his mother had given him up out of her great love for him and not for any other reason. I could never have Andrew think his mother sold him for a fistful of money, or worse, that I bought him with a fistful of money.

"Yes, I think you would be good for my boy," she said, her voice cracking. "Very good."

Little did I know at the time, Dana had been offered $5,000 by another couple for the boy only weeks before. Despite her abject poverty, Vio persuaded her to turn the couple down.

"I didn't have a good feeling," Vio admitted later, thinking about that offer. "But I wasn't really sure about you, either," he said with a grin, "especially after I found out you were a preacher. The only preacher I had ever met was Orthodox, with a cross and a beard and a black funny hat. But you acted more like a comedian."

We talked for hours. Dana asked about our family, our house, and our children. I shared about my ministry, how I had come to meet her son, and our deep love for him.

Finally, Dana dropped her head to her chest as tears began to fall. Wiping at them with the back of her hand, she tried to smile.

"Yes, I think you would be good for my boy," she said, her voice cracking. "Very good."

With that, Vio and Dana followed us down the three flights of stairs to the car below with Daniela. I wanted to sing, to shout, but I contained myself by catching Chrissie's eye. They were ready to help us make Andrew our own!

After spending another night at the motel in Arad, we picked up Dana, Vio, and Daniela to start the wheels in motion. The 40 mile drive from Dana's dormitory to the orphanage seemed to take hours. Finally, we drove down the little alley to the building where Andrew and the other children were housed.

It was another warm fall day with a bright sun against the bluest sky I have ever seen. After parking, Vio headed into the building in search of Andrew. The rest of us followed the chain-link fence surrounding the building, glancing at the yard, which was nothing more than a barren patch of dirt—without a single blade of grass and with no toys, no benches. After realizing that Andrew was not inside, Vio came back and joined us in the yard.

> And then Andrew did something breathtaking.
> He smiled.

We found all the children sitting outside on tattered blankets, making games of throwing the colored leaves up into the air and watching them dance to the ground.

The children were laughing. Imagine that—these orphans who had nothing were laughing at the pleasure of a few fall leaves floating through into the wind. I had to chuckle at their joy. But I quickly noticed that Andrew wasn't among them. I scanned the grounds, anxious to find my boy.

Finally, Dana and I spotted him at the same time on the other side of the yard. A blue wool cap was pulled tightly down on his head, and he stared off into the distance, not seeming to notice anything around him. He sat alone next to a rusty pipe, with no leaves with which to play.

I grabbed Chrissie's arm and pointed, then pulled her along with me toward him, my heart pounding. His blank face continued staring off into the distance as we approached. I stood beside him, and after a moment, he looked up.

Those green eyes melted me in an instant. I just wanted to hold him, wrap my arms around him. I wanted to take him to the car, to a plane, and to Alabama, where he belonged. My son. He was my son.

Vio reached down, pulled Andrew into his arms, and turned to introduce him to Chrissie.

Chrissie pulled off the blue cap as she took the boy into her arms. My heart dropped. They had shaved him bald! Every hair on my boy's sweet head was gone. It was gone! Why had they done this to my Andrew?

Tenderly, Chrissie rubbed his naked little head, and as she held him for the first time, her face had the same glow as when she delivered our two children. In her heart, at that moment, in that filthy place, Andrew was born.

I watched as she placed one of her small hands on each side of his face, the photo on our refrigerator coming to life in her arms. He blinked and slowly turned his face to hers. Time froze. His piercing green eyes focused on her face, her hair, and finally her eyes.

And then Andrew did something breathtaking. He smiled.

This hungry, bald, abandoned boy smiled, not at the woman who had given birth to him, but at the woman who was in an instant his mother.

As mother and child got to know each other, I sat down inside with the orphanage worker I had met before. I had left her money—$100, three months' wages—and begged her to promise that she would find answers for me to confirm that he could be adopted. My efforts had gotten me nowhere, so I'd stopped calling her a few months before. I knew that I would make no real progress until I was physically in the country again.

When I walked in, she glanced up and then back down at her paperwork. Then she looked again, startled, like she had seen a ghost.

"Mr. Cameron, hello," she said. Glancing behind me, her face registered surprise at the sight of Dana and Vio. "I did not expect you."

"What have you learned about the boy?" I asked without the usual pleasantries. "My wife and I are here with his birth mother to do whatever is required to adopt him and take him back to the States. We have her permission; she'll sign anything she needs to. What can you tell me?"

The woman looked pale, nervous.

"We thought...I thought...well, it's just that Andrew is scheduled to be reassigned on..." Her voice trailed as she checked her calendar. "Yes, right here. In three weeks, he will be picked up and transferred to another facility."

The woman was talking about my boy like he was a UPS package! Someone else's UPS package! Picked up? Transferred? Another facility? Where? Why? The questions rattled in my brain faster than I could process them, much less get them out.

"You see, Mr. Cameron, the boy turned four last Monday. That is the cutoff age at this institution. We are preparing him to be moved, and," she said as she shuffled through her papers, "there is no way to help you. There is nothing here about where he is going, only what date and time he is to be picked up, October 21 at 11:00 a.m."

"There is no way," she repeated. "No way."

How could she be telling me that they were taking Andrew away to God knows where and I couldn't do a darn thing about it?

"There is no way," she repeated. "No way."

This boy meant nothing to her, and I meant even less. She was an agent of the government, one of the seemingly countless faceless, heartless souls who spent their days mindlessly following rules and orders. The boy's fate had been dictated by the strike of a pen. Done. Finished.

The silence between us grew awkward. I cleared my throat and shifted in my seat.

"Excuse me," I finally said. "I am not giving up. That is my boy. I didn't come halfway around the world to be turned away like this."

I stopped talking, my mind racing ahead. She was the only link I had to the people making the decision. Even with Dana's permission to take the boy, I still could do nothing. Andrew could be lost forever in the bowels of the Romania orphan system.

"But you didn't lose him," the Lord spoke to my rapidly beating heart. "He is here. You are here. I am here." As His words soothed my spirit, the words of a praise song I'd sung all my life came into my heart:

I know the Lord will make a way for me.
I know the Lord will make a way for me
If I live a holy life, shun the wrong, and do the right.
I know the Lord will make a way for me.

With renewed faith that God would indeed make a way for me, I demanded to see someone in charge. Less than an hour later, we stood in front of yet another worker, a tall blonde supervisor with the charm of a rabid pit bull.

"Have a seat," she motioned as she launched into her speech. "Mr. Cameron, these children are in our care. We can't let just anyone take them. We'd have to have a government official grant permission for such a thing," she said as she pushed back her chair and stood. "Only the mayor himself could grant that."

Silence filled the room. Chrissie took my hand and squeezed it. She didn't have to tell me what she was thinking—I could tell by the look on her face.

"Thank you so much for all your help," I said as I glanced down at the papers the woman had given me. "Could you kindly direct me to the mayor's office?"

Our trip to the mayor's office—a small, ugly, two-floor building with tiny windows—was my next glimpse into the dysfunctional government that was now running this post-soviet country. There was no money to provide the people with even the most basic services that they'd had in the past. Mother Russia no longer backed the country's power and control, so the government sought to hang onto power through intimidation and rudeness. And it was darn good at it.

Inside, a young woman, dressed in the same dull brown as her surroundings, sat at a metal desk in the foyer. As we walked up to her desk, she ignored us as she continued to rapidly read through the stack of papers on her desk.

Minutes went by. Chrissie cleared her throat. I rattled the car keys, tapped my foot on the tile floor. Dana and Vio held hands as they stood behind us, and Daniela went off in search of a ladies room. The woman kept reading, stopping only to pick up a pencil and mark a few words in the margin. Finally, she turned to what looked like the last page, finished it, filed it, and then looked up with a face filled with boredom.

"Yes?" she asked.

"We're here to see the mayor," I said. "We've traveled a very long way to get here."

When it was clear that the distance we'd traveled did not impress her, I told her that the fate of a small orphan child rested in our hands and of the supposed wealth we had as Americans. I felt like Dorothy and the Scarecrow outside the gate of the Emerald City.

There was no way, she said, that we would be allowed to see the mayor.

Her words hung in the air: No way. No way.

With that, she spun around in her chair until her back was facing us, and started digging through a tall beige filing cabinet.

I stared at the back of her head, and we waited. Again the minutes passed by. Finally, she turned, surprised to see us still standing there.

Over the next four hours, I talked my way not only past her, but also past several other higher levels of secretaries and managers. Finally, I sat down with the man himself—the mayor of this seemingly godforsaken city—and explained through an interpreter what I wanted to do.

> Hours later, through the grace and providence of God, I had a note in my hand—permission to take Andrew out of the orphanage!

I saw heads shaking, people frowning, and heard the words, "No way" echoing in my head, yet still in my heart I heard, "I know the Lord will make a way for me."

Hours later, through the grace and providence of God, I had a note in my hand— permission to take Andrew out of the orphanage!

Chrissie and I hurried to the car before the mayor could change his mind. I peeled out of the parking lot, gravel flying and my wife laughing. Dana and Vio sat stoically behind us, wide-eyed.

We had it; we had permission to take the boy! We were one step closer to claiming this child as our own, against all odds! I'm not sure if there were speed limits in Romania, but if there were, we broke every one of them getting back to the orphanage and getting Andrew back in our arms.

Less than 30 minutes later, we were walking past a very shocked orphanage worker as she read the permission slip one more time. She didn't think we'd ever get the mayor to sign off on us taking the boy out—why should he? But as we walked out with Andrew in our arms, that song danced across my heart again:

I know the Lord will make a way for me.
I know the Lord will make a way for me
If I live a holy life, shun the wrong, and do the right.
I know the Lord will make a way for me.

NO WAY

THERE WERE NO CAR seats in Romania then (in fact, I doubt many people have them now), so Chrissie climbed into the front seat beside me with Andrew in her arms. Dana, Vio, and Daniela all climbed into the back.

Wide-eyed, Andrew looked around the car in awe, and it suddenly occurred to me that this poor child had never been anywhere but in the orphanage or the yard, and he certainly had no concept of what a car was. He didn't know us, didn't understand a word we said. His eyes were wide like saucers, not from fear, but from curiosity.

As I started the car, music from the radio filled the air. At once Andrew began bouncing up and down to the tune, so excited that I was afraid he would hurt himself. Puzzled by the sound, he bent down and put his ear to the speaker, rocking his bald head to the beat. He had never heard music before.

His smile was beyond anything I can put into words. My heart was so full I thought I would burst. He was here, right here, in the car with us! What a miracle!

Thanking God, I put the car in reverse and backed out of the drive. Andrew continued to bounce to the music, and Chrissie reached to the back of the car and pulled out a two-liter bottle of Pepsi. Before she could get a cup or try to communicate and ask if he was thirsty, Andrew grabbed the huge bottle and put it to his lips.

> This poor child had been dehydrated his entire life.

Chrissie and I watched, dumbfounded. This tiny boy drank the entire bottle in a matter of minutes, stopping only once for air. I had never seen anything like it!

Then I remembered what one of the workers told me: The children were given only a tiny bit of water each day so they would not need to urinate very often. The less urine, the fewer diaper changes or trips to the potty. Either of these outcomes meant less work for the caretakers. This poor child had been dehydrated his entire life. I shook my head at the thought, the inhumanity, and started down the road.

My mind wandered as we started aimlessly down the street. A motel room would cost at least $70, and I had maybe $25 left. How could that motel get away with charging $70 a night for such a dirty, little room?

"It's because we are Americans," I reminded myself.

Rich Americans—I laughed aloud at the thought. So rich that we were homeless. It just wasn't fair. If we had been guests of a local company or church, I knew the motel would only charge $3. But since we were Americans...

Suddenly, everything became clear. A church was the only place in town that I knew anyone—the very church that my dad and I had stopped at the first time we came to Romania six months before. We had loaded all of our food, all the medicine, blankets, and formula into its warehouse. By the time the church "discovered" the orphanage a stone's throw away, everything was gone. The church had given it to its own starving people.

I looked around for a place to turn around. Surely the church would help. It would cost it nothing to book the motel—we could pay for it; we just needed it booked in the church's name.

I smiled at the beauty of the plan. It was perfect. God was in control. I put a bit more pressure on the accelerator, and 20 minutes later we were pulling into the familiar parking lot. The truth was, I hated to ask the church for anything, a seed of resentment still in my soul over what had happened.

I looked at Andrew's face, the picture of an angel, then at Chrissie, Daniela, Dana, and Vio. I had no choice. I was desperate—too desperate to let my ego stand in the way.

I left the others in the car and was relieved to find the church door unlocked.

"Hello," I called, "anyone here?" My voice echoed down the empty halls. I walked across the parking lot, over to the warehouse, the "scene of the crime." To my relief, there were a few workers. I didn't know any of their names, but I recognized a few of the faces.

After taking a deep breath, I started making my case:

"My name is Philip Cameron. I live in America and was just here a few months ago. Maybe you remember," I said. "We brought a huge tractor-trailer filled with food and supplies. I was a rich man that day, and I had many things to give your people.

"Today I am flat broke. I have nowhere to stay. My wife is waiting for me in the car with a little boy we are trying to adopt. If the church would book us a motel room—which we would gladly pay for—it would only cost $3 a night. But if I book it, they charge $70. I am exhausted. I have no money. Please, can you help me?"

The men looked at one another. It was easy to tell that they'd understood enough of what I said to know they wanted no part of it. Why would they help me? I had nothing to give them.

No one would look at me, each shaking his head in a silent, "Sorry, but no."

I started to protest when a voice boomed from behind me.

"Philip Cameron!"

Turning, I was met with the biggest, most welcome smile I have ever seen. It was Ion, the man I had met years before who asked for the James Dobson books.

"Thanks for the books," he said, grabbing me in a bear hug. "You have no idea what a blessing they have been to the ministry."

He stood there staring at me like I was a returning hero. "What brings you back here, brother?"

I motioned for him to follow me outside, out of the earshot of the others. After finding a few chairs for us to sit in, I told him all that had happened from the time we left the goods at the church to the many legal dead ends we'd faced in trying to adopt Andrew.

"My friend, I am out of money and out of ideas," I said. "We have no place to stay and less than a quarter of a tank of gas. I have hit a wall. Can you help me? Do you know any way to help us? Anyone?"

I looked at him, and he looked, well, embarrassed.

"Ion? What are you thinking? You know someone, don't you? Tell me, please!"

He cleared his throat, "Philip, I am the only Christian in my family. I share my faith every chance I get, but so far, nothing. My sister…well, she is the mistress of the vice president of the court."

The enormity of his words washed over me, and my heart leaped in anticipation of what he would say next.

> "Meet me tomorrow morning at the courthouse, and I will make it so the vice president of the court will see you; he will not say no to me."

"I am not sure why the church will not help you book a room, but I have a better idea," he continued. "I have a flat not far from here. It's small, but my wife and I can go and stay with my in-laws, and you can use it as home base for a few days. I'll take you to meet my sister, and then we can go to my home. I can't promise my sister will agree to help, but it is worth a shot."

The ride across town seemed endless (as nearly all of the trips had). I was anxious to meet Ion's sister, hopeful that she would be able to help us. As she came down to meet us at the car, I was immediately struck by her presence. She had an hourglass figure in a Mae West kind of way. Her long dark hair fell over her pale shoulders in waves, setting off her rich brown eyes. Her arms were long and thin; her nails painted a bright red. Her voice was deep and throaty; her manner, almost abrasive. Everything about this woman screamed for attention and control.

She dressed unlike anyone I had seen in Romania. In a world where everyone wore black and brown, her dress was a vivid shade of blue, tight, and cinched at the waist with a large leather belt. She stood perhaps five feet, five inches in her tall heels and may very well have been wearing the only pair of panty hose in eastern Europe.

As soon as we told her our story, Ion's sister began to cry. "I will do whatever I can to help you," she said, with Ion translating. "Meet me tomorrow morning at the courthouse, and I will make it so the vice president of the court will see you; he will not say no to me."

The next morning, we arrived at the court. Hundreds of people lined the halls. We followed behind Ion's sister as if we were lost puppies, not knowing where we were going. After what seemed like hours, she opened the big padded door at the end of the hallway and walked in. Ignoring the two secretaries who sat guarding the inner office, she flung open another door, unannounced.

> Finally, we had hope. We had a plan. We had help.

There sat Cristian Dacu, vice president of the court. I had no idea what he would say, how he would react. I stood behind Ion's sister, not understanding a word she was saying to him. I was surprised when he looked over his high desk and asked, in perfectly clear English, where in Alabama I was from.

After listening to our story, he said, "Normally, there is a six-week waiting period for the mother. Do you think she would allow that to be put aside?"

"I know she would, yes."

"Come back on Thursday at 2:00," he said. "The boy will need his birth certificate, too."

Less than an hour later, we returned to Ion's tiny flat. Ion's wife made us a cabbage and pork soup and served it with thick slices of crusty bread. I ate like a man spared from execution.

Finally, we had hope. We had a plan. We had help. I couldn't stop thanking the Lord, praising Him. I couldn't stop smiling at my pretty wife, tickling that boy who would soon be mine.

CHAPTER

THE END OF THE LINE

WHEN CHRISSIE, DANIELA, AND I arrived at Ion's that night, I placed a call to my office in America and got Ministry Coordinator Brian Paterson on the phone. I had a handful of dedicated, hardworking staff members—low-paid, but loyal to the core. None was more long-suffering than Brian.

"Brian, I need you to overnight us some more money," I said as soon as he answered. "We've gone through almost everything we have, and I have no idea how long we'll be here."

"Well, I don't know what to tell you," Brian stammered. "Things aren't good here either. I'm not sure what Lisa can scrape together to send to you. Honestly, we are about at the end of the line. I'm not sure how we are going to survive this."

> Static filled the line as he fell silent.

See, there was a problem, and it was a big one: If I was not preaching in churches every Sunday, the ministry didn't have any income. These trips to Romania were not exactly in our budget, nor was the loss of income while I was away. I had been gone a week, with our return nowhere in sight, and I was down to the last few dollars in my pocket. I needed him to send money right away.

"How bad is it?" I asked, but the truth was I knew before he said a word.

"Things are pretty grim around here," Brian sighed. "I wasn't able to make payroll yesterday because the money just isn't there. I gave everyone a few dollars for groceries and gas, but it won't last long. You didn't take your last paycheck, remember, so there isn't even money in your account to pay your mortgage or anything else. I am hoping they don't turn off the lights."

Static filled the line as he fell silent.

Daniela had offered for us to stay with her and her mom in Bucharest, and we had no choice but to accept. Frankly, up until this point, she had been useless beyond some simple translations. I didn't trust her, didn't like her, and not simply because I was judging her for her planned abortion; everything about her seemed fake. I wanted to get away from her, but I had little choice.

Closing my eyes, I began to pray silently. It was all starting to look impossible, yet I knew what the Lord was telling me to do. Brian promised to make a few calls and do the best he could, but he sounded utterly defeated, uncommon for a man of faith like him. I didn't have the words to encourage him and, after giving him Daniela's address to send the money to, ended the call as quickly as I could.

In an effort to forget the call, I tried to focus on the day ahead. It was time to pay a visit to Dana's mother. I was more nervous about asking her for Andrew's birth certificate than I had been about meeting Dana. Dana told us story after story of her mother, and I knew that she had no love for Andrew, that she had no compassion for her daughter. She refused to even meet Andrew when he was born, and I knew that a woman who was capable of calling her own grandson a bastard was also capable of preventing us from taking him, just to spite Dana.

When we were let into the apartment, Dana was immediately led away by her mother to the kitchen, and I could hear her howling in tears through the thin walls.

The woman said nothing to persuade Dana to keep Andrew, but her actions said it all. She came out of the kitchen and sat beside the boy, stroking his head, kissing his cheek. I knew if we stayed there, Dana would never let us take Andrew; her mother would persuade her to keep legal guardianship of him while he suffered in the orphanage.

I silently begged God not to let that happen. A clock on the mantel ticked loudly as the minutes passed. I could not understand anything being said between mother and daughter, but there was a peace that began to settle in the room, a presence that I could almost see. Finally, the older woman stood, shook her head, and walked out of the room. When she returned, she handed a small brown envelope to Dana, kissed Andrew's head, and disappeared back into the kitchen.

> We had the final document we needed!

We had the final document we needed!

The next day, we had a court session. As in every Communist court, there were five judges, dressed in robes, lording over the proceedings. Just seeing these formally attired men made my heart skip a beat. We had come so far. If they didn't give us permission to take Andrew, I would be forced to give up. They were the final rule in Romania; there is no court of appeals. There would be nowhere left to turn.

The whole process was a blur, as if I were watching it from afar, not taking part in it.

"The social study's waived?"

"Yes."

"Who is giving this baby up for adoption?"

Dana stood up, "I am. I am the child's mother."

"Who is accepting this child?"

Chrissie and I stood up, "We are." I looked over at Chrissie, and she was wearing a look of complete serenity.

"Lord Jesus," I prayed, "move against all odds on this situation."

Bang! The gavel came down; the vice president of the court was on his feet, and Ion's sister looked like the cat that swallowed the canary. Daniela smiled.

"He is yours," she said, smiling.

Chrissie and I jumped up and down, screaming with joy at the news that Andrew was our boy at last. Right there in the courtroom, I planted a big kiss on Chrissie's smiling face. I even managed to hug Daniela. Still beaming, I turned to hug Dana and Vio, too.

The look on Dana's face was a strange mixture of sadness and happiness, confusion and realization. Vio, on the other hand, was easy to read. His face was dark, like storm clouds had passed over him.

It dawned on me in that moment that this news meant the end for Dana, Vio, and this boy. They were losing him forever. As long as he was in the orphanage, there was always a chance, however slim, that one day they would be a family. Now, all hope was gone.

We headed to the car, and Vio climbed onto the backseat with Dana. Each reached out to the other for comfort while Daniela leaned against the door on her side. The sun had set, and a dark stillness blanketed the car. No one said a word as I started down the street toward the edge of town and began the journey back to Dana's dorm.

Andrew was starting to tire and was snuggling into Chrissie's arms to sleep. Chrissie hugged the boy close then handed him back to Dana. As a mom, Chrissie was keenly aware that this was the last chance Dana would have to feel the warmth and joy of her child sleeping in her arms.

It seemed for a moment Andrew would relax and sleep in the back with her, but suddenly, he bolted for the front seat.

"Mommy!" he screamed, struggling with all of his might to climb back into the front to Chrissie.

All week, we had been working with Andrew to bond Chrissie to him as his mother, and it had worked. I didn't hear Dana crying as the child settled back into Chrissie's lap to sleep, but I knew she was. How could she not be?

Chrissie and I were anxious to drop off Dana and Vio and head with Daniela to the Embassy in Bucharest to get our son's passport and start our new lives. But at the same time, I was painfully aware of the anguish that every mile brought to the couple behind me. One mile closer to our having the boy. One mile closer to their losing the boy.

With Chrissie and I being from one country, living in another, and adopting a toddler from a third, the next vital step was to get a passport for Andrew that would allow him out of Romania, through the countries in our path, and finally back home to America. If you have never traveled outside the United States, it is almost impossible to explain how important a passport is. That little booklet proves to authorities all over the world who you are, where you have been, and what permissions you have regarding entering and staying in other countries. Passports aren't given at birth, and people generally don't get them until they need to travel. Without a passport for the child, none of the hurdles we had overcome would matter. Andrew would be stuck in Romania.

> Wordlessly, Chrissie and I quickly jumped back in the car and started on our way.

Finally, we were back at Dana's dormitory parking lot. It was dark, with only a single street lamp to help light the way. A burning pile of garbage cast a yellow glow over everything. I stopped the car, started to unload the few things Dana and Vio brought, and turned to say our good-byes.

"You will be good to the baby?" Vio asked as we stood behind the car. I nodded. Of course.

Chrissie handed Andrew back to Dana for a final hug. Sobbing, she rubbed his fuzzy head against her cheek, breathed in his sweet baby smell as if to engrave it on her heart. Again we reassured them that we would love him and that he would never want for anything, and we promised a Christmas picture and update every year and that I would visit when I came back to Romania.

"Take care of my baby," Dana said as she handed the child back to us. She quickly turned away from her only child, burying her head in her hands. Vio enveloped her in his arms.

Wordlessly, Chrissie and I quickly jumped back in the car and started on our way.

I looked back as we drove away. I couldn't stop myself. Dana was crying uncontrollably on the pavement, clutching her stomach, the pain of losing her child too great to bear. Vio stood off to the side, his face buried in his hands.

In that moment, I felt like a criminal. But again, I heard in my heart, "I know the Lord will make a way...."

As the words of the song soothed my spirit, the dam of emotions within me burst. I was driving while sobbing hysterically. It was a miracle I didn't hit anyone or anything because I was completely on autopilot.

I didn't know north from south, east from west; all I knew was I had to put distance between Andrew's birth mother and us before I could relax in my spirit. I don't mean that harshly; I loved Dana. But my heart was so attached to Andrew. I just wanted him to be mine forever.

Realizing I had not been paying attention and had no idea where we were, I heard myself pray out loud, "Lord, if I am headed the wrong way, will you let a fox run across the road?"

Now, mind you, in all my trips to Romania, I had never seen a fox in the road. Not once. Where this prayer came from, I had no idea.

A darting motion caught my eye. It was a small gray fox, its tail as long as its thin body. It started out, glared into my lights, then quickly passed in front of my car and disappeared into the woods on the other side of the street.

I grinned at Chrissie, did a quick U-turn, and headed out of town, with tears still wet on my face, but a grin as well.

After driving all night, we finally arrived at Daniela's the next morning. I was exhausted from the trip, but also wired, a ball of nervous energy, anxious to move this process along.

The building she lived in was one of six in a sad complex of three-story buildings. We unloaded the car and followed her up the stairs, my mind suddenly fixated on the thought of a hot shower and a clean set of clothes.

Trash littered the stairway and halls, and an unpleasant smell permeated the building. Daniela turned her key into three different dead bolts and let us in with a series of clicks.

I looked around at the place she was living in with her mother. The floor was a dull vinyl, devoid of color, and I could just make out the faintest track of some floral pattern on the faded wallpaper. Where pictures had once hung there were only nails, and dog poop and hair littered the floor.

It seemed to be a main room with a tiny kitchenette off to the side and a bedroom in the back. A chipped bowl sat empty beside the sink, along with a box of what looked like breakfast cereal. As best I could tell, it was the only food in the house.

After dropping my bags near the door, I set off to find the bathroom, carefully skirting around the dog poop, which seemed to be everywhere. In the tiny flat, the bathroom wasn't hard to find, but it was the strangest I had ever seen. The room was small—so small that I could touch the wall in front of me, the wall behind me, and the wall to my right, all while sitting on the toilet.

Stranger still, the showerhead was mounted on the wall above the toilet, and the drain was at my feet. The entire room was the shower stall! I could have dealt with that okay, but there was no water. Apparently, water would get turned on from time to time, often in the middle of the night, and everyone would jump up, get a shower, fill the sink, and then go back to bed.

Since there was no water, I quickly gave up on the thought of a shower, and walked gingerly back to the living room, trying to avoid stepping into anything vile.

Daniela took what money I had left and went to the corner market to see if they had any eggs, meat, or bread—anything—to buy.

The apartment only had two small windows and two dimly lit lamps. Chrissie and I were assigned the one private bedroom, and I put on my pajamas and crawled into bed. After the few days we'd had, I thought going to bed would be easy, but I was wrong. At the end of the bed, Chrissie sat staring at me, bouncing Andrew in her arms.

A phone call? Who the heck knew where to find me?

"Aren't you coming to bed?" I asked, stifling a yawn.

"Philip Cameron, have you not noticed that this place is filthy? I bet she hasn't washed those sheets in years! Look! See that? Fleas! The bed is crawling with fleas!"

Ignoring Chrissie's complaints, I took the boy from her and leaned back. His skin was damp with sweat, and the smell of urine clung to him like a blanket. He peed all the time and had no control at all over his bowels. But I held him close and rocked him, feeling the fleas stinging my skin.

Suddenly, there was a knock on the door.

"Philip," Daniela's irritating voice came from the other side of the door. "You have a phone call."

A phone call? Who the heck knew where to find me?

I passed Andrew back to Chrissie and stepped out to take the call. "Hello?"

"Philip Cameron!" the familiar voice of an old friend came through the line. It was Bob D'Andrea, president of The Christian Television Network (CTN) in Clearwater, Florida.

"Philip, you are on the air! You were supposed to be here with us tonight...."

I groaned inwardly. That appointment was one of the many that I had canceled to come and get Andrew.

"So," he said, "how are you doing?"

For a moment, I hesitated. I was raised to give a good report. After all, God is always in control. But the words of great news and high hopes were far from my lips.

"Brother Bob," I muttered, "things are bad. I am trying to adopt a baby in Romania, and while doors keep opening, there are so many of them. This is taking forever. The government is a nightmare. We have no gas for the car. I am out of money, so we can't afford a motel. I have no idea if we will even have supper tonight. There is no food."

A few minutes later, after I complained in even greater detail, we ended the call. I returned to the bedroom and climbed back into bed with the fleas.

Turning to Chrissie, I said, "Well, that is one program that I'll never have to worry about getting invited back to."

I rolled over. Somehow I slept.

> The people gave. And $20,000 came in and saved my ministry and my house, and allowed me to stay and fight the good fight for my boy.

It was only later that I learned that as soon as I hung up, Bob looked directly into the television camera and talked to the people in his live audience, broadcasting all over Florida in real time.

"Friends, we have to pray, and we have to do something to help Philip and this little orphan boy. For the next 20 minutes, we are going to pray, and as we do, I am going to ask you to go to the phone and call in a gift. Every penny you give in the next twenty minutes will go directly to help Philip Cameron."

He prayed. The people gave. And $20,000 came in and saved my ministry and my house and allowed me to stay and fight the good fight for my boy. It was a miracle, but I slept without knowing it.

The next morning, I awoke with hope that we would be able to get a motel room and escape staying another night in that filthy dump.

Daniela's mother handed us a plate of food; apparently she'd been able to get some bread and meat. I was too hungry and too broke not to eat a little of it.

As we ate, Daniela disappeared behind the closed door of the bedroom and then came out with a big smile on her face.

"Look," she said, "a package for you."

It was easy to tell it had already been opened. Inside, all I found was a note from Lisa, a handful of candy, and $2.

"Where is the rest of it?" I demanded.

Daniela looked bewildered. I wasn't stupid. Lisa had not sent me an overnight package with only $2 in it!

I looked past Daniela long enough to see her mom pick up a piece of ham from the floor—dog poop, hair, and all—and place it on Chrissie's plate. Disgusted, I stood up. It was time to go. I'd sleep in the car before I'd spend another night with this con woman and her mother.

Turning to Chrissie, I quietly said, "Let's go. These people aren't helping us. They are stealing from us."

Not knowing how to get to the Embassy, we left Daniela and her mother behind. I could not stand to spend one more day with those women, and there was no way I was going to let them steal from me again.

CHAPTER

THE BABY WITH
NO COUNTRY

V IO HAD WRITTEN OUT directions to the American Embassy on the back of an envelope. There were no street signs, so I had to rely on his crudely drawn map, counting out the number of streets we needed to pass before turning left or right.

"Is that a street or an alley?" I'd ask Chrissie as we passed, as if she would know.

We finally found the building after a few wrong turns and false starts. I have always loved the sight of the American flag blowing in the breeze, but never more than at that moment, seeing it there marking the American Embassy.

> In that moment,
> it meant hope.

In that moment, it meant hope. People would understand English. They would share my concern for this child. We would not be alone in this fight anymore. My passport was my ticket to help, and I needed it desperately.

As I stepped inside the Embassy, it was as though we had left Romania entirely. The floors were gleaming white with thick carpets. Impressive paintings hung on every wall. Glass vases filled with fresh flowers sat on massive wooden desks. Looking down at my wrinkled clothes and dull shoes, I suddenly felt very out of place.

"May I help you, sir?" the woman at the front desk said with a slight New England accent.

I stepped up to her desk, introduced myself, and explained, "We are here because my wife and I live in America, and we really need some help. We have green cards, but we are British citizens. This little boy, Andrew, is an orphan. We would like to take him back to Alabama."

The lady dropped her head and peered at me over her thick glasses. "Sir," she said with an air of disgust, "what are you doing here?"

"Pardon me?" I asked, confused.

"This is the *American* Embassy," she said. Behind me I heard Chrissie start to cry.

"You are not American," the woman continued, as if we hadn't heard or understood her the first time. "You are British.

> I was stunned. Everything about the woman had totally rattled me to the core. I was speechless, stunned, frozen in place

I have no idea what you are doing here or what possessed you to think you can adopt a Romanian child. There is no way I can help. Good day, sir."

I was stunned. Everything about the woman had totally rattled me to the core. I was speechless, stunned, frozen in place.

Mustering up courage I didn't feel, I said, "You will see me again," and I turned on my heel, put my arm around Chrissie's tiny waist, and led her from the building.

By the time we got to the door, her body was heaving with sobs. I looked at her red face, wet with tears, those eyes I loved puffy from so little sleep. I heard in my heart: "I know the Lord will make a way...."

I was overwhelmed by the gravity of the situation; we had come so far, overcome so many obstacles. All I could do was take our case down the street to the British Embassy and pray the Lord would pave the way. Moments later, another flag of red, white, and blue waved in the breeze—the British Union Jack—marking the building as property of my motherland.

Inside, the British Embassy was as stately as the American, filled with good-looking men and women in their tailored suits. An L-shaped desk with the most modern Selectric typewriter I had ever seen sat in the foyer. A smart-looking woman was pulling a form out of her machine and turned to greet me as I approached.

Once again, I introduced myself and told her why I was there. I drew back, expecting some taunt or reprimand. Instead, the woman stood and extended her hand, "My name is Thelma. Just where in the U.K. are you folks from?"

Startled, I stammered a bit. "It's such a wee place, I doubt you have heard of it. Peterhead, Scotland. It's up..."

She cut me off, "Aye, I know exactly where Peterhead is; I grew up not far from there myself!"

For a moment we bantered back and forth like old friends, talking about the places we missed, foods you could only get back home, people we might have known in common. Just by hearing a kind voice, sharing a bit of home, I felt that hope was being rekindled. It was refreshing, like a cool drink of water.

Finally, Thelma noticed someone behind me waiting for her attention.

"You will need to see my boss," she said, hurrying us along as she waved the next couple forward. "Her name is Christy Gordon-Rowe. She is tied up right now, but if you will have a seat, she'll be with you very soon."

Turning to Chrissie, I saw that her eyes were still clouded from crying. I could tell the slightest setback would cause her to melt into a puddle of fresh tears.

Suddenly, the halls echoed with the wailing of a grief-stricken woman. "No!" she cried. "You can't take him! He is mine! I have cared for him since the day he was born. If you won't give me the papers, I will smuggle him out!"

Hearing the raw pain in the woman's voice was all Chrissie could stand. As the details of her story poured out in torrents of tears and screams, it was clear that the woman had more claim on her baby than we did on Andrew. Yet she was still being denied the right to take him to her home in Canada.

> After excusing herself, Chrissie took Andrew to a bench in the back of the room while I waited for the meeting, feeling powerless and alone.

After excusing herself, Chrissie took Andrew to a bench in the back of the room while I waited for the meeting, feeling powerless and alone.

It was years before I learned what had happened when Chrissie sat down on that bench. She dropped her face in her hands and began to weep uncontrollably. As she cried, her heart was too wounded to even pray. All hope was gone.

Her love for Andrew was so deep, so pure, and she couldn't imagine life without him. She couldn't imagine loving him so much and having to leave him in that orphanage again. As her sobs turned to silent tears, she felt the warmth of two hands on her shoulders. The hands were large, firm, reassuring. Chrissie gasped but was afraid to open her eyes. She was afraid that the feeling, the very real touch she felt on her shoulders, would disappear.

When she finally opened her eyes, no one was there. No one she could see, anyway. But she knew. She knew Jesus was with us and that Andrew would be our son.

Meanwhile, the esteemed Ms. Gordon-Rowe greeted me. Stone-faced and hard, she didn't even have to open her mouth before I knew she would not be helping us.

She talked to me like I were a dim-witted boy. "Mr. Cameron, I don't know what made you think we could help. You live in America. The baby is Romanian. There is nothing I can do for you."

And without as much as a good-bye, she walked back to her office and closed the door with a thud.

I was crestfallen. I stood frozen in my tracks. It was the end of the road—we'd have to leave him here, back at the orphanage. Then I thought of Chrissie. She was already a mess. How would she handle one more rejection, one more dead end?

Andrew was still fast asleep as I walked up. Looking at Chrissie, I could tell something had changed, that she had changed. There was a sparkle in her eyes I had not seen in days. I hated to tell her the news and spoil her mood, but I had no choice.

"Chrissie, they can't help us either," I started. "We live in America."

"That's okay, we have all the help we need," Chrissie said with a boldness that rocked me back on my heels. She grabbed the baby buggy, and we headed to the car. We didn't say a word as we loaded the car, but I could make out the faintest of tunes as my wife folded up the buggy for the truck. Was she humming the tune of "I know the Lord will make a way for me"?

The British Embassy rejected us; we weren't living in Britain at the time, so it had no say in the American matters. And the American Embassy wouldn't even let us in anymore because we weren't American citizens. All we had were our American green cards and Andrew with his Romanian visa. We were at a loss.

But Chrissie's sudden calmness centered me. Moments before, my thoughts had drifted to what it would be like, feel like, to take Andrew back to the orphanage, fly home, and start over.

Now I knew better. In spite of all the setbacks we had faced, God was in control. The only thing I knew to do was drive to Vienna in preparation of our return to America and trust that He would make a way for us to take Andrew home with us.

We arrived in Vienna that afternoon at 3:40. I knew it was getting late, and I told Chrissie, "Let's go to the American Embassy. I know it didn't work in Romania, but let's give it another shot."

The minute the words came out of my mouth, it occurred to me that we wanted to go to the Marriott. To this day, I don't know how I knew that, but the urging in my spirit was clear. It turned out that the American Embassy was on the fourth floor of the same building that housed the Marriott.

Despite this happy coincidence, we had no idea what to expect as we walked up to the Embassy. Would they be able to help us, or would they just turn us away like the embassies in Romania had? Would they even let us in?

> As soon as the words spilled out, I shut up and let God do the rest.

We got inside and explained our situation, just like we had so many times before. "Hello, my name is Philip Cameron, and this is my wife, Chrissie. We've just adopted this boy from Romania...."

The brutal response crushed my hope that we had come to the right place. "What have you done to this boy? You have ruined his life. You have made him a nobody; he has no country now. There is nothing we can do!" the man shouted at me.

I would not be moved by his words. God sent me to this place, and there had to be a reason.

Raising my voice, I demanded to see someone in charge. "You do not know what this boy has been through, the hell he has lived in his entire life—starved, abandoned, neglected to the point of child abuse. I want to speak with your supervisor now. My son will come home with me to America."

As soon as the words spilled out, I shut up and let God do the rest. I didn't know what else to do. I was at a dead end, completely out of ideas.

Then, from behind, a tall young man stepped forward. With his short, cropped hair and formal manner, he looked to be in the military, but his voice was kind.

"You know what? There might be a way," he said.

My heart stopped. I think Chrissie's did as well.

He continued, "We've got a provision in American Immigration Law. It's called Humanitarian Parole, and it states that if we feel that somebody has suffered enough, we waive all the regulations and give the person humanitarian parole."

And that is exactly what they did.

Now he was ours, really ours. We were on our way back to our house.

We'd come to Romania to spend a week; we'd stayed for more than a month. We put everything we owned on the line, in faith believing that what God said to my heart was true, that this was our little boy.

Several days later, after miles of red tape, we finally heard the roar of a jet plane beneath us. Chrissie was tired, but glowing like the new mother she was. She had dressed Andrew in little green corduroys for the trip home to meet his new family.

> We put everything we owned on the line, in faith believing that what God said to my heart was true, that this was our little boy.

Everything on the plane fascinated him. He figured out early on in the flight that if he stood on the armrest between us, he could reach the bright orange buttons above.

His motor skills were not as developed as a four-year-old boy's should be; he had been "caged" for too long. But still he scrambled to see all, touch all.

Two switches controlled the lights. Off. On. Off. On. The light switches were great fun, but the best was the red button. It summoned the flight attendant—not that Andrew cared—who would come, roll her eyes, turn off the button, and return to the galley. But he loved the alarm it sounded. Though we tried to interest him in other things every hour he was awake, it was a lost cause.

When we landed at the Atlanta airport eight hours later, Andrew's eyes were as wide as saucers as he took in his surroundings. The sights and the sounds enthralled him. Elevators, escalators, ice cream, telephones ringing, pagers beeping, hamburgers, little golf carts zipping back and forth. For a child who had spent four years in a rusty metal crib, there was so much to take in!

When we pulled into our driveway in Montgomery, Alabama, that November day, a sign, decorated in bright primary colors, fluttered against the front of the house declaring "Welcome Home, Andrew!" It was one of the happiest sights of my life.

Inside, my dad awaited our arrival. He had come over from Scotland to help with the ministry while we were away and refused to leave until his new grandson arrived.

I sat down on the sofa, put Andrew on my lap, and invited his new siblings and grandfather to get to know him. They tickled him, showed him toys, did everything they could to make him laugh.

Philip Jr. and Melody both had their own bedrooms, and we planned to convert the small study into Andrew's room.

"No way!" 11-year-old Philip Jr. said when he heard our plan. "My new brother is staying in *my* room with me!"

Over his shoulder, I caught Chrissie's eye and winked. It was good to be home. It was good to have my boy where he belonged—almost too good to be true.

Hours later, with everyone in bed, I sat watching the last of the embers glow in the fireplace. Silently, I thanked the Lord, praising Him for His goodness, for His mercy for all of us, and especially for my Andrew. I shuddered thinking about where he had come from— the smells, the neglect, the lack of food and water.

"The others are still there."

Where did that thought come from? My mind was racing back and forth. Andrew was here, safe.

The other little faces still in those "cages" flashed before my eyes. Andrew was rescued. The others were not. How would I ever be able to look at Andrew and not think of those other orphans?

Then, I realized that was exactly what God had in mind.

CHAPTER 11

TV MEETS ORPHAN

ANDREW. MY SON.

Having him in our home after so many months was such a treat. He greeted me each morning with those green eyes, wide as saucers, filled with delight.

His progress in overcoming his developmental delays was slow but steady. Every struggle he had in holding an object, putting together blocks, or even just walking was a reminder of what he had been through. Watching him took me back to Romania, to the rusty metal cribs, the rows and rows of neglected toddlers.

> Watching him took me back to Romania, to the rusty metal cribs, the rows and rows of neglected toddlers.

With Andrew as my daily reminder, it wasn't long before I climbed on another plane back to Romania, determined to do more to help the little ones we'd left behind at his orphanage.

Every few months for seven years, I traveled back there and fixed roofs, painted walls, replaced cribs, and brought food, diapers, formula, and medicine. Chrissie came with me as often as she could, but with a house full of little ones, it was difficult.

On one of my first trips back, just as I was about to take off from the London airport, I called Chrissie one last time. I wanted to check in again before being incommunicado for a while.

I had just gotten her on the phone when she barked, "I'll talk to you *later*" in a huff.

My sweet wife never talks like that, and I knew better than to let it drop.

"You will tell me now," I said softly.

Silence. Then another huff.

"I don't know whether to kill you or congratulate you. I am pregnant!"

I almost dropped the phone. "You are pregnant?" I asked, pretending I hadn't heard her correctly.

"Pregnant."

I had forgotten for a moment that I was not traveling alone. Brian Paterson was standing behind me as I repeated the words back into the phone.

"You are pregnant?"

> But when sweet Lauren entered the world six months later, there was no doubt that she was God's plan.

The snickers behind me became more than I could ignore. Brian doubled over, screaming with laughter. Mr. Two-Kids-Only. Yeah, right! I could have smacked him.

I tried to make peace with Chrissie before hanging up, but I didn't get too far. After saying our good-byes, I hung up the phone and turned to face my "friend."

Brian's face was red, his cheeks wet from laughing so hard.

I found no humor in the situation. It seemed that overnight we would go from two children to four. After all, we had just adopted Andrew six months before. Who says God doesn't have a sense of humor?

But when sweet Lauren entered the world six months later, there was no doubt that she was God's plan. While she stole my heart as only one's baby girl can do, she also provided unexpected help for Andrew. From the moment we brought her home, Andrew was smitten with her. As she grew, he began to imitate her, developing alongside her and overcoming the last of his delays. It was a plan that only God in His wisdom could have designed.

Chrissie was really stuck at home now while I continued to divide my time between Alabama and Romania.

Overseas, I worked 16-hour days, cramming as much work as possible into each trip to Romania so I could be home as often as possible.

I found one resource that made my trips far more productive: Vio. Yes, the boyfriend (now husband) of Andrew's birth mother.

I made a point to call on Dana on my first trip back to Romania after bringing Andrew to Alabama. I found Vio and Dana living in an apartment that was totally empty, with not a stick of furniture, not even a bite of food. All they had was a nasty-looking mattress on the floor of the one room and a tiny white hamster in a cage in the corner.

They were shocked to see me, even though I had promised to stay in touch. I brought with me a small video player and showed them clips of Andrew's progress and growth. Dana's face lit up as she watched her boy chasing our dog across the tiny screen, playing with his brother and sister. Most of all, she couldn't get over his face, how round it was, how healthy, how happy he looked.

My intention was to have a short visit and leave their cupboards filled with food and, if I am disclosing all here, a few cartons of cigarettes as a gift. But Vio volunteered to stay with me a few days and help with the language barrier or customs, or just add a few muscles to the team.

It was an offer I couldn't refuse, and I've thanked the Lord many times that I didn't. Vio knew his way around officials and could be charming or intimidating as the need arose. He could play the "heavy," and I could be the "dumb" American or Brit or whatever they thought of me as. It worked. And Vio became my go-to guy there in eastern Europe.

We started with the most basic needs—food, new beds, a working heating system. I hired contractors, marshaled volunteers, brought people and resources from Scotland. Slowly, the place began to show signs of real life. The children grew healthier; the workers came to care more. It was expensive, but worth every dime.

Between trips I traveled from church to church, from telethon to telethon across the United States. It was the ministry's only real source of income to pay for the work with the orphans.

I would tell Andrew's story, detailing the suffering of countless babies who were still stuck in those cribs, and ask God's people to help me.

One invitation brought me to a telethon in the Midwest. I was one of several speakers lined up to help raise the necessary funds for the station—the only Christian television station in the area—to broadcast the gospel, long before cable television.

In the green room, I sat down with a cup of tea and soon was joined by one of the other guests. The man was well-known in Christian circles at the time, bright, charismatic, and engaging to listen to, and he had an impressive track record for raising funds.

He asked about my work, and I casually began telling him the story. We talked for more than an hour, and the more I shared, the more passionate I became. The man sat at the edge of his seat, tearing up as I told stories of the children I met, the conditions in which they lived.

I paused as my mind brought me back from all that we had seen to the most immediate needs I was facing in the next few weeks to renovate the next orphanage.

As I sat in the richly appointed room, my flight was less than a month away, and I was still tens of thousands of dollars short to tackle the next phase. I had no clue how I was going to get that money, but I knew that God was in control.

"When are you going next?" he asked, interrupting my thoughts.

I told him the dates.

"I am going with you," he said without hesitation. "We will make this happen!"

He was quickly on the phone with his executive secretary, putting together a team of videographers, photographers, and various other workers right before my eyes! I was blown away to think that a professional team finally would see what I saw and be able to tell the tale. The concept had never occurred to me before! I was too busy spending every dime on roofing materials and contractors that it had never occurred to me to spend money on marketing.

Before I knew it, I was in Romania with him and his crew. We were up at sunrise the first morning and on our way to the next orphanage we planned to help. Everything about this place was as bad as that from which Andrew had been rescued. I cautioned my guest and his crew about what to expect, knowing full well my words could not begin to express the horror they were about to see. The people nodded their heads solemnly. "We'll be okay," they seemed to say with their expressions.

We unloaded the truck, and the team got in position. Video cameras in those days weighed about 30 pounds, lighting had to be a higher quality, and on-air talent had to speak into a handheld microphone to be heard.

As soon as all systems were optimized, the crew started toward the building, with cameras rolling.

"I am standing here outside an orphanage in Romania, a small country in eastern Europe that was once part of the Communist regime," the man spoke into the microphone. "For many years, no one knew what was happening behind the borders of this country. Her people are poor, the jobless rate is over 50 percent, and bread and meat are scarce even if you have money to pay for them. This is a country where they throw away their babies."

He artfully stopped speaking and let the grave words sink in.

"Parents abandon their babies like yesterday's newspaper. They are thrown away in a trash heap or at a neighbor's house, or left in the hospital beds they were born in. What happens to these babies... hundreds of thousands of innocent children? Let me show you...."

He dropped his microphone from his face, and the videographer signaled, "Cut."

Wow, I thought, *that was powerful.*

I could see the value in using good media to tell the story and was excited to see how this turned out.

The team gathered its equipment and started for the building door. The talent got the signal to begin, and he looked into the camera one last time with the door closed behind him. Pausing for effect, he closed his eyes for a second, and then he threw open the heavy metal door, letting out an audible gasp as he did so.

> His voice trembling with emotion, the man began going from crib to crib.

As he walked in, still facing the camera, his eyes filled with tears as the smell of urine overwhelmed him. The crew coughed into their elbows to muffle the sounds from the video. With the cameras rolling, the man started to speak, though I had to strain to hear his words.

His voice trembling with emotion, the man began going from crib to crib.

"There must be a hundred babies in this room, and there is not an adult in sight. This little girl, poor thing, look at her. Someone chopped off all her hair. Why is she naked? Can't someone at least put a diaper on this child? She is so thin I can see her ribs," he called over his shoulder.

"Look, she is trying to grab my finger, but she is too weak. And this little boy. What is wrong with him? Look at those bruises. He could not have done this himself, could he? Dear Lord. And this one...."

Crib to crib, room to room, the video continued. I watched for a while, but I needed to get some other work done. Forcing myself to focus, I sat off in the corner with a notebook as he taped, jotting down the items I needed to purchase in town that night. Light bulbs. Skin cream. Sixteen windowpanes to replace those that were broken.

His next segment interrupted my thoughts: "I need your help. It will cost $200,000 to make this place livable for these children. Just $100 will pay for a new crib with a soft mattress, a warm blanket, and real sheets. Just $300 will replace a single window—and we have 20 that must be replaced before the bitter winter descends on these babies. It will cost $50,000 just to fix the roof."

Brilliant, I thought. *No wonder he is a "star" in Christian circles, and I am just the guy buying the light bulbs.*

From there we went across town to the home where I had found my Andrew. It was the first home we helped, and it was so different that I hardly recognized it. The floors were new and sparkling clean, and there were new cribs, new linens, and bright toys with which the children could play. The children were well-fed and diapered, and a row of plastic potty seats lined the wall under the new windows. The television crew members were tired when they arrived, but jumped with life at what they saw. Now this was a story!

I beamed with pride as they documented the great work that had been done. The talent took one well-dressed child after the other in his arms, his moving commentary flowing with no script or cue cards.

"It is amazing what a few dollars from generous people can do. Look at these new windows. These children have nothing to fear this winter. The roof over their heads is new." On and on he went about all the great things God's people had done.

Soon, the light of the day began to fade. I was out of energy myself, and I would sleep well that night knowing that the need was well-documented, that others would share my burden for these kids.

The next day, I saw the crew off to the airport. We hugged and shook hands, and I was told to expect to hear from them shortly.

I returned to my work on both sides of the ocean. Days turned into weeks; weeks to months. Finally, I was back in Montgomery, enjoying a simple night of family time and television.

As I surfed from one channel to the next, the man's face suddenly filled my 19-inch screen. Behind him was the Romanian orphanage. I leaned forward in my easy chair and turned up the sound. I listened first with interest, then with horror. The man was on the air taking credit for all the work we had done and asking for money to do more. His 800 number and address were on the screen. The closing announcer said there was no time to lose.

> The man had taken advantage of His orphans, not mine.

It was the closest I came to hearing from the man or his crew again, and I certainly never saw a penny of that money. I can't say if the children of Romania did either.

I was tempted to call him, hire a lawyer, and threaten him, but the Lord would not let me. Sure, I nursed resentment, but anytime I dwelled on it for too long, the Lord would convict me that this was His work, not mine. The man had taken advantage of His orphans, not mine.

My job was not to call this man out; my job was to keep doing what God called me to do. So I threw myself even deeper into my work.

The next trip I had planned was for the first week of January. As I was preparing for my visit, Chrissie was just starting to un-deck the halls from our family Christmas.

It dawned on me that while our holiday was over, Christmas had not yet come to Romania. The country was steeped in the traditions of the Orthodox Church, and Christmas is celebrated on January 6— exactly when I would be there.

The thought excited me and quickly turned into a plan. I would get to take Christmas to orphans who had never had gifts in their lives. What a treat that would be! Chrissie, the kids, the staff, and every friend I had flew into action. Dolls, toy trucks, bouncy balls, pretty ribbons, candies, and more were packed into boxes and loaded into my car.

That year was the first of what has become a tradition, evolving into tens of thousands of shoe box-sized plastic bins that we hand-deliver to children back at the orphanage we first transformed—Andrew's "home."

Soon, the Christmas boxes became the icing on the cake in our work with orphans. As we focused on one home after the other, we got to know the children.

By returning annually to each home after all the reconstruction had been finished, we could make sure everything was being properly managed and check on the children. Plus, it was great fun.

Throughout the next seven years, we worked in Romania, improving conditions and the lives of countless children. By then, either our ministry or another had targeted every orphanage we could find in the country, and conditions drastically improved for the orphans of Romania.

In December of 1996, I arrived in Scotland to pick up Christmas boxes for my annual trip. Dad met us en route.

"It is time to move on," he said. "This year, when you go to Romania to deliver Christmas gifts, keep going. I want you to visit Moldova."

Moldova? I had never heard of Moldova, much less thought of visiting there.

"Where is Moldova?" I asked.

"It's just one country away," my dad replied. "Just keep driving when you get to Romania."

To make sure I understood that he meant business, he handed over a newspaper article on Moldova's orphanages. The headline read "The Dying Rooms of Moldova." Though it was hard for me to comprehend, the writer described conditions far worse than any I had seen, even in Romania.

I read up on the country and learned that this tiny country, about the size of Maryland, was once part of the Russian Empire. Prior to that, it was under Romanian rule. During World War II, German and Romanian troops attacked the Moldovan SSR and the Ukrainian SSR, and Romania regained the territory. However, in 1944, Soviet forces occupied the small country, overthrowing the Romanian leadership.

When the Iron Curtain fell, many thought it would again become part of Romania; after all, they shared the same language and much of the same history and culture, but the leaders decided to become an independent nation. It quickly became the poorest nation in all of Europe.

The level of poverty in this small nation is beyond the comprehension of most Americans. We have no problem visualizing the poor in Africa, in Haiti. We have seen enough videos and photos to picture the small stick huts with dirt floors and no water or electricity.

But this is Europe! How can this nation have the majority of her people living in mud houses, without electricity, using bathrooms that are just holes in the ground behind the house? But that is the reality, and to make matters worse, in winter the temperature drops as low as twenty below zero.

Through research, I learned that this was a Third World country by any standard. And my dad was sending me there as casually as you would send someone to the corner store for a gallon of milk.

On the trip down, the snow was shoulder-high, and the journey took me across the Carpathian Mountains on the narrowest, most dangerous road I had ever traveled.

The only thing I can compare these mountains to are the cartoon mountains in "How the Grinch Stole Christmas!" They seemed to go straight up into the sky, and the tiny road wound up and down them with no guardrails at all. The snow was piled up on the sides so high that it was hard to tell where the road ended and the snowbank began.

I was driving a small rental car, and the truck behind me was now light after distributing all of the Christmas gifts in Romania. There were no streetlights, and there was very little traffic. I had fleeting thoughts that if the truck were to go over the edge and down into the snow, no one would find us until the spring thaw.

But onward I drove. Vio said little, but I had found it to be normal. His English, to put it kindly, was rudimentary at best. We communicated in the simplest of forms. "Food?" *"Da"* (Yes), and he'd point to where I should stop to eat. "Gas?" *"Da."* He'd jump out to fill the tank.

Finally, we made it to the border of Moldova. I had a map of the country and the location of one of the orphanages. It was in a village called Hincesti.

We arrived around noon at the doorway of the building that would change my life forever. It was another typical building "designed" by the Communists, box-like and painted an ugly shade of tan.

The bitterly cold wind lashed my face as I opened the door and stepped out onto the driveway. Looking more carefully at the building, I saw that the windows were all broken; some were missing entirely with nothing left but rotten frames. I shook my head in disgust. It looked like it had been decades since anything was painted or repaired.

Garbage littered the walkway, and the smell made me nauseated. Discarded clothes, shoes, papers, broken toys were all piled up in random heaps in the snow.

I walked through the door and braced myself for what I would find. It didn't help. The familiar smells of urine, filth, body odor, and garbage overwhelmed me. I pressed on, hating every moment, but knowing full well that this was an appointment the Lord had ordained.

As I walked in, I shook the snow off my shoes. The director, Mr. Ciubottari, met me at the foyer. A short man with a red face and dark eyes, he shook my hand and welcomed me without even a hint of shame at the conditions of the place. I looked past him and saw dirty blankets nailed over the broken windows in a feeble attempt to keep out the cold.

> "Have you ever seen a baby freeze to death?" he repeated.

The children in this home were all handicapped, and they huddled together in the middle of one large room. Each was wearing layers of mismatched and ill-fitting clothing. It looked as though they had been handed a pile of clothing with no regard to its condition or size, and they were wearing every single bit of it just to stay alive.

The room was frighteningly quiet. Even though there were several children in front of me, no one said a word, made eye contact, or acknowledged I was there at all. Each child stared off into space, a few rocking and a few asleep in their chairs. It was the most hopeless collection of children I had ever seen in my life.

The director broke the silence. "Have you ever seen a baby freeze to death?"

I stopped and turned. "What did you say?"

"Have you ever seen a baby freeze to death?" he repeated.

CHAPTER

STELLA

"Have you ever seen a baby freeze to death?"

The words hung in the frozen air. Had I ever seen a baby freeze to death?

I looked at him, stunned.

He continued, "Already 16 children have frozen to death this winter."

It was only December 6!

The thought of these helpless children was more than I could deal with, and I couldn't get the words or the image out of my mind as I toured the building. First, he showed me the equipment used to heat the facility. Of the three coal-fired boilers, only one worked, and it didn't work well. In fact, it looked to be about a hundred years old.

It required coal, of course, but the coal bunker was empty. The tiny flame that danced inside was quickly disappearing as it devoured the few twigs and branches someone had tossed inside.

"Last year, 30 children froze to death here," he added offhandedly. "All of them died in their beds."

Touching the metal beds in the subzero weather was like touching a flagpole outside during a winter storm. If I were to touch my tongue to the bedpost, it would instantly freeze. I couldn't imagine a worse way to die than with raw skin affixed to frozen metal.

Every room of the dreadful place was freezing, every child was listless, and his or her eyes were vacant. The only movement I saw was when lunch was placed in front of the children. Each child grabbed the plate and ate the tiny bit of gruel as quickly as possible. I could not recognize anything on the plate other than a few grains of rice, but they lapped it up like hungry dogs.

> If these children stayed in these conditions, if another one froze to death, it would be my fault.

I struggled to make sense of it all. I was less than a day's drive from some of the world's most powerful economies, and children—even babies—were freezing to death in their beds, starving, without any hope at all!

To make matters worse—if that was even possible—these children were not just orphans; they were also handicapped. Some were blind. Many were in wheelchairs. Some were mentally disabled. What a cruel life!

The director interrupted my thoughts. "The children would like to sing for you."

They started to sing a song, and I recognized the tune. The words in English are:

This is the day, this is the day
That the Lord hath made, that the Lord hath made
I will rejoice, I will rejoice
And be glad in it, and be glad in it

My heart melted at the familiar tune. I could not keep an emotional distance from these children, even if I wanted to. God had brought me into their lives to change them, to show them His love. I could no longer simply curse the Communists, the bureaucracy, their parents, the director, or staff; I had to do something.

If these children stayed in these conditions, if another one froze to death, it would be my fault. I had seen this, experienced this, and knew firsthand how bad it was. These were not children in a book or magazine; they were in front of me, singing their hearts out, so cold that their lips were blue.

Vio translated as the children sang another song, and I started asking the kids questions and telling them a little about my family and me. Suddenly, a girl in the front row caught my eye.

Clearly, she was older than most of the children, almost a foot taller. But she was bent over and held her badly deformed right arm out from her body in an unnatural way. Later I would learn that when we walked, she dragged her right leg behind her, and she suffered from terrible epileptic seizures.

"My name is Stella," she told me.

We began the first of what would be many conversations over the years to come. I liked this girl. She had an amazing spirit, a personality that was larger than life. It was clear to see the other kids looked up to her as a leader, and I understood why.

She was very bright and a wonderful conversationalist, asking great questions about me, my family, and my travels. Her personal story was as sad as any I had ever heard. Her father abandoned her mother with six children. With no way to support them, her mother had no choice but to turn them all over to the state rather than watching them starve to death.

Some of the other children listened as Stella shared her story, but most slipped away to their rooms. Stella and I talked for what seemed like hours, and she finally asked me to follow her. Down the darkened hall we went until we were at her room. After pulling a small bag from under her pillow, she emptied the contents on the bed.

Two tapestries were unfolded as she lovingly displayed her work for me. They were remarkable, really, especially given her handicap. They must have taken months to create.

Smiling, I reached out to touch the soft fabric, to admire the delicate work. "These are beautiful," I said.

"You take one," she said. "I want to give one to you!"

Never in my life has anyone given so unselfishly to me. She was literally giving me half of everything she had in this world. I was honored beyond words. I was also smitten. This girl would be more than just another orphan I would help. She would become my lifelong friend.

> She was literally giving me half of everything she had in this world.

I would be back to see her, and soon. No one would freeze to death in this building again, not as long as I had breath in my body. And Stella would have all the sewing essentials she needed to make more tapestries!

After I folded the work of art over my arm, I led her back to find the director. Sitting in his office, I could see my breath as I talked. Vio interpreted as the director explained that during the worst night of the year, he had moved all of the children into a single room so they could stay as warm as possible. By daylight, seven of those children were dead.

I looked at Stella and started making a plan with Vio. Could we get coal with my credit cards? Could we board up the broken windows until we could buy new ones? We had to move, and we had to move quickly.

We did what we could that week, and then I made the fastest round trip I have ever made to America and back. I preached at a few churches, called in every favor I had, and then jumped on a plane back to Moldova.

Days later, there was a roaring fire in the furnace. The children were no longer in danger, and as long as I could supply $1,800 a month for coal, they never would be again. Stella met me at the door with a huge grin.

We spent the day together, and she proved to be my best assistant and guide. It was the second of many, many visits.

Like I had done in the Romanian orphanages, I started working alongside a team to transform this state-run orphanage into a real home. Once the most basic needs—heat, windows, and food—were met, we were able to bring Christmas gifts.

The kids began to recognize our truck as soon as it was in sight. I'd open the door to the sounds of delighted children calling, "Philip! Philip!" Their cries would alert Stella of my arrival, and she'd meet me at the door, help me hand out gifts, and direct the children as she went.

Over time, our work was matched by work from other nonprofits in Europe. The building was completely remodeled, and the children had the best living conditions they'd ever known. I was so pleased to see the positive change. I knew Stella and the others would always be part of my life and part of my visits and Christmas runs from Romania to Moldova, and I didn't have to worry about any of them freezing to death.

But it was time to move on to the next chapter in my life and ministry. We opened a Christian campground, Brigadoon, back in Alabama, and were rejoicing at how the Lord was using it to bring young people to Christ. That work in Alabama seemed a fitting next chapter for my life and work.

The Singing Camerons L to R: Cousin Robert, Cousin Eileen, myself, my mother Wendy and my father Simon.

I had much to smile about, engaged to the most amazing girl.

My bride took my breath away then and more so today.

Simon and Wendy Cameron, the finest parents a man could have, standing next to the Rolls Royce we rented for £40 for our wedding day.

As I neared Andrew's crib, God told me, "This is your son."

As an orphaned and handicapped girl, Stella had nowhere to go when she aged out at 16. She was dead from HIV by 19.

Daughter Melody is joined by the orphans of Cupcui on our first visit.

I kept coming back to visit them, just like I promised I would.

On left is Galina on our first stop to Cupcui. Today she lives in the same building, now totally reborn and refurbished as Providence House. She serves full-time, welcoming new orphans, teaching Bible stories and sharing Christ's love.

The young men of Simon's House act as mentors to the young boys at our orphanage as well as the state-run orphanages.

Every summer a dozen or more girls from Stella's House tour churches across the US, Canada, and the UK sharing their amazing testimonies.

Galina today (right) with friend Stela Slanina (left)

Happily ever after for my son Andrew and his beautiful
bride, Natalie.

The girls of Stella's Voice with Andrew and Natalie on their wedding day.

CHAPTER 13

"WHAT'S THAT SIGN?"

IT WAS A WONDERFUL feeling knowing that the "heavy lifting" part of my work in Moldova was over. A corporation in Europe finally adopted the orphanage where Stella lived in Hincesti and rebuilt it from top to bottom. I could rest easy knowing that the children would always have heat and a solid roof over their heads.

I planned a "fun trip."

This was a new concept to me, to go visit the orphans in Moldova and just bring Christmas gifts. I felt like Santa himself. Someone else was now providing the heat, and I would feel the joy of being able to put all my efforts into bringing Christmas cheer to the children.

It was 2003, and I was able to bring Melody and Andrew along with me. It would be a great treat for them—and for the orphans—to play together, to discover each of the toys in the boxes and to learn how to play with them. Traveling over, I was in a great mood.

The trip itself was uneventful. We flew to Scotland with a Tom Valley, a doctor from Columbus, Ohio. He was a new friend and supporter, a tall man with a bald head and gold wire-trim glasses. He was a likable character with an easy smile. His personality made the time pass quickly.

When we landed in Scotland, we met Willie Moffatt, a rather crusty old truck driver who often volunteered for Dad's ministry, picked up the truck filled with little plastic boxes of toys, and drove the 2,000 miles to Romania. There, we picked up Vio and then made our way to Moldova in yet another snowstorm. I was anxious to see Stella and the others and have a big old-fashioned holiday with my kids and the orphans. We had hot chocolate, candy canes, and lots of special treats that would be new for the kids.

> At the end of the visit, Stella limped beside us to the door, the last to say good-bye.

At the end of the visit, Stella limped beside us to the door, the last to say good-bye. I hugged her tiny frame to me and wished her a merry Christmas one last time. As we started down the road away from the orphanage, I let my mind wander. I would now have more time with my family, more time to preach, more time to study. Life would continue at a much calmer pace.

Heavy snow began falling, but it seemed fitting. It was Christmas, after all, and the truck was warm. There was only one final stop to make, a few more gifts to deliver.

As the weather got worse, though, I wondered how many hours the weather conditions would add to the trip. Traveling with my kids, there was always the constant chorus of, "When will we get there? Are we there yet?" from the backseat. Other than that, the only noise we heard was caused by the truck hitting the frequent potholes.

The sky was gray and dim; it was as though the world outside the truck was a black-and-white photograph. The snow was deep and piled high on either side of the road, and the landscape offered only bare, dark trees swaying in the winter wind.

Behind me, Willie flashed his lights. Tapping the brakes, I slowed, knowing that if I stopped we would get stuck.

Tom pointed and asked, "Philip, what's that sign?"

I glanced at the large blue-and-white sign that said "Casa de Copii Orfani"—House for the Orphan Children. An arrow pointed to a tiny road, barely visible in the snow.

"Oh, no," I said, shaking my head. "I am not going there." I knew better than to look and see. No way was he talking me into this.

"We are here, Philip. Come on, let's take a look."

I would not be persuaded. It was time for a bit of logic.

"Look at the snow; are you kidding me? We'll get this truck stuck in the snow, and we'll be walking back to Scotland. We have one more stop to make. Let's just get this done and go home."

> There was only one problem: We had to pass that sign again on our way back out of the country.

With that, we continued down the road once more. Hours later, when the last remaining boxes had been delivered, all I wanted to do was go home and start a new, simpler chapter in my life. There was only one problem: We had to pass that sign again on our way back out of the country. Sure enough, Tom was not going to let it pass without an argument.

Finally, he wore me down enough to go along with it. I figured we would get out, decide the road was too narrow, and keep moving. I signaled for Willie to pull over and waited for him to walk over to us. All three of us looked up the road where the sign pointed.

"Willie, tell the man. We can't get up that road. It is crazy," I retorted.

Willie interrupted, "No, no. We can do this. Let's give it a go."

Then Andrew piped up. "Come on, Dad, let's go see. What's the harm?"

"I need to stretch my legs anyway, so let's go see what's up there," Melody added.

There was no point in trying to fight them all.

So up the long road we went. As soon as we entered the village, we saw a large building, again with all the hallmarks of a Communist-designed institution. The ugly, drab building with a flat roof looked like a giant box with little square windows sitting in the snow.

It was almost dark, but there was a faint light coming from a few of the windows. For a moment, I thought the building might be abandoned. We parked anyway and started up the broken steps.

As I walked through the front door, I was overwhelmed with the same toxic smells of filth, urine, garbage, and poor hygiene.

Here we go again, I thought, suddenly feeling very tired.

The place was as bad as, if not worse than, any place I had ever seen. Black mold covered the walls, and there was no light at all in the foyer. There was no one in sight, but down the hall I heard singing.

Curious, we walked toward the source of the music and soon entered a large room with more than 100 children huddled together in two groups. One group was on the left side of the room, and the other group was on the right.

It was the strangest thing. It was like they were giving a concert, but there was no audience. No mothers or fathers or friends. In fact, the few adults in the room wore expressions of either sheer boredom or outright disgust. They were obviously only there because they were paid to be; it was nothing more than a job.

In all of my life, I had never seen anything sadder. These children were celebrating Christmas the only way they knew how, by taking turns singing to one another in this dark, dingy room. Not a single parent was there to cheer them on; all they had was one another and their songs.

Immediately, the children went silent as they noticed us walk in. I am sure we scared them at first, as they did not know what to expect from us. The room was freezing cold. Some of the children didn't even have coats.

"No, please, sing, sing!" I motioned with my hands as Vio spoke up behind me in Romanian, encouraging them to sing again.

Andrew and Melody followed our lead and began to clap and repeat Vio's words: "Sing! Sing!"

Looking at one another in surprise, the children began singing again, this time a bit louder, happier. After each song, we clapped like crazy, encouraging them, trying to show how delighted we were with the music. We didn't understand a word they were singing, but we were determined to be the best audience we could be.

"Be their dad."

As I smiled and listened, my mind was racing. All the Christmas boxes were gone. I had no more toys, no more candy, nothing left to give these kids. My heart sank at the thought.

Then, out of nowhere, I heard the words, "Don't just bring them things. Be their dad."

I looked from face to face, child to child. These kids were beautiful, sad, hopeless, and forgotten.

"Be their dad."

How could I possibly do that? Repairing roofs and windows was one thing, but being a dad is a whole different kettle of fish.

After the singing, I set about getting to know as many of the children as I could in the short time we were there. One of the first kids I reached out to was a pale girl who looked to be about 14. Her hair was a soft brown, and she had a cute upturned nose, like a button. I later learned her name was Galina.

She was one of the shyest children in the room, hanging back in the corner. I had to draw her out to get her to interact with me. She was a sad, broken little thing.

During my next visits, it seemed she always had a cleaning rag in her hand; she was trying to busy herself, I guess. The others would push her toward me, and she would duck away. As I got to know her, it was plain to see that there was something terribly, terribly wrong with her. She squinted all the time. She struggled to see. Every now and then, she would make a face, like a flash of pain had hit her in the head.

> Galina was the youngest of six children.

Galina was the youngest of six children. When her parents divorced, Galina was only four. Her mother took some of the children, her father took the others, and for reasons Galina will never know, she was left behind.

Galina, this tiny slip of a girl, was left in an orphanage for preschoolers with more than 200 other little ones. Like the others in that part of Moldova, she spoke only Russian.

The home was short-staffed, and the staff, short-tempered. Galina quickly learned to be the invisible one in a sea of toddlers. She was hungry and cold, but her heart was fixed on one thing—seeing her parents again. But they never came, never wrote, and never called.

Meanwhile, adults regularly visited the orphanage in search of little ones to adopt. Galina was one of the few whose parents never signed over parental rights. Because of that, she could never be adopted. One by one, her friends were adopted, and once again, she was left wondering why she was the only one left alone.

So not only did she feel the pain of abandonment, but she also had no hope of escaping the orphanage and being part of a real family.

Before she was ready to enter grade school, workers loaded her into a car and drove her to the orphanage at Cupcui. She didn't know a single child. She only spoke Russian, and everyone else spoke Romanian.

One of the orphanage workers immediately sat Galina down and told her that she would learn to speak Romanian during the summer, and if she didn't, she would be beaten until she did!

But worse, she was overwhelmed by the fact that now her parents would never be able to find her; they would not know where to look.

Every day for this little girl was a nightmare of shouting, threats, and relentless beatings. Somehow she learned to read and write enough to be ready for school in September, but that started another sad chapter of her life.

> In Moldova, the worst thing you can be is an orphan.

In Moldova, the worst thing you can be is an orphan. Orphans are hated, despised, treated like they are less than animals. But they are still sent to attend public school with the village children, who often called the orphans names and made up nasty songs about them. Teachers looked the other way, and the director of the orphanage didn't care.

The rules were harsh for a little girl as scared as Galina. If she was late getting back to the orphanage and lunch was over, she'd have nothing to eat until supper. The workers would taunt her, making sure she knew they were taking her food home to feed their cows and pigs.

At Cupcui Orphanage, the conditions were even worse than in the orphanage where she was first kept. The roof leaked, and her bed was often wet at night. She and the other girls would try and push the beds around to find a dry spot, but it was a useless endeavor.

It was also cold. The windows were broken, the heat didn't work, and little Galina stood beside me with no coat, just a few layers of dirty sweaters.

And God told me to be Galina's dad.

Despite her shyness, Galina was never far away from a dark-haired beauty named Constantia. It was clear these two were fast friends, closer than sisters.

With high cheekbones and sparkling eyes, Constantia was striking, but filthy. Her curly hair was a short mop, like a boy's haircut, that looked like it had never been washed.

She was quiet like her friend Galina, with an expression that was haunting—a little girl who had seen too much pain in her short life. The more I learned of her story, the more my heart broke.

Her father had been murdered by some orphaned teens when she was only four years old. He was a shepherd and was coming home from the hills where his sheep had been grazing all day when the boys jumped him, robbed him of what little money he had, and left him for dead.

For three days, the man struggled to get home, crawling in the mud as rain dripped into his open wounds. Constantia's mother realized something was wrong when the sheep started finding their way home without him. Finally, he collapsed on the doorstep, and she rushed him to a hospital, but it was too late.

The morning of Constantia's father's funeral was the last time she would wake up in her own bed. By nightfall, she was at her grandmother's house, and her mother simply walked away, leaving Constantia and her older sister Cristina without so much as a good-bye.

For two years, the grandmother tried to raise the girls. Although she loved them, she was desperately poor. In time, they were forced to eat chicken feed just to survive. Constantia's grandmother desired to give the children a better life, so with good intentions, she told them that their mother was dead and put them on a bus to the orphanage.

It was hard to imagine anything worse than what the two girls had already experienced. But it did get worse. The sisters were separated due to their age difference and six-year-old Constantia was left alone in a roomful of strangers.

Her one blessing was the few good friends she had made. Over the months, she began to accept that this was her life—she was nothing but an orphan.

A year later, a frightening woman showed up at the orphanage calling her name. Constantia turned to look at her and was scared by what she saw. The woman was bruised, dirty, and visibly drunk.

"I am your mother," the woman insisted, but that made no sense at all to the little girl. Her mother was dead; her grandmother had told her so. Who was this scary woman?

But it was *her mother, and she took Constantia and her sister out of the orphanage and moved them to Ukraine to work in a convent. From the time she was seven until she was eleven, Constantia was not allowed to go to school. Instead, she was forced to work alongside her mom with the farm animals. At night, her mother would drink until she passed out—until the people at the convent found out.*

Overnight, they were homeless with no jobs and nothing to eat. Within days of traveling back to Moldova, her mom found a boyfriend and moved into his house. The man was violent and did not like children. When Constantia's mother drank, he would get angry and beat her then throw all of them out on the street in the middle of the night.

Boyfriends came and went, but abuse was a common element in all of those "relationships." During those months, Constantia was always hungry, and her boots were so small that her feet ached all day, making it nearly impossible to walk.

One night, one of the men got so angry that Constantia and her mother went running out of the house in the middle of

> And God told me to be her dad.

the night and into a cornfield to hide. They heard something hit the ground near them and saw the glimmer of a knife blade sticking out of the ground.

Being sent back to the orphanage offered Constantia a better life, but by the time she returned, she was crawling with lice, and the workers warned the other girls not to sleep in the same bed as her. Embarrassed, Constantia could not even look the other girls in the eyes.

But one girl, Galina, took her hand and whispered, "I will share a bed with you; I don't care if you have lice."

Galina became her safety net. In the four years Constantia had spent in Ukraine, she had forgotten how to speak Romanian and spoke only

Russian. Galina spoke both languages, but due to her eyesight, she struggled, too. Being the two older kids kept in classes with children much younger, the girls helped each other with their studies.

Still, Constantia struggled to understand why her mother didn't love her, why she had sent Constantia away. The only thing that made sense was that she was too ugly and stupid to be loved.

And God told me to be her dad.

Years later, she told me that the day I met her, she was so sad it felt like she had a "black heart." She wondered, as she had wondered every Christmas, how come even Santa Claus hated orphans. Why did he bring presents to everyone but orphans?

She also had been thinking about her mother a lot. As she was singing in that cold little room with the other orphans, she imagined that her mother was in the audience clapping, beaming with pride at her performance.

And it was in the midst of that longing that we showed up.

Before we left that day, I wanted to give them something, anything. All I could do was cheer them on as they sang. Finally, I remembered I had some little stickers in the truck, and I rushed out to get them.

Years later, Constantia shared how much that silly little sticker meant to her. "I kept it on my face for days, just touching it and remembering that someone smiled at me and gave this to me. I didn't understand why you came, why you seemed to like us, since we were nothing but orphans. But it was a wonderful Christmas present."

I was stunned to feel so deeply about these children so quickly. I felt like they were mine.

The last thing I did before I left that day was tour the facility so I could see the whole place. I began to make a list of what structural things needed to be accomplished to make this orphanage livable.

There was not a warm spot in the whole building. The showers were outside in another unheated building with nothing but a steady drip of cold water coming from the faucet. In the warmer months, five girls at a time were allowed a five-minute shower. In the dead of winter, they didn't bother; it was just too cold.

In Moldova, the government closes the orphanages in the summer and sends the children back to their families for "vacation" or to other families that are each paid 11 cents per day to keep the children. Most of these children who are placed in families for pay are put to work on the farms, tending sheep, weeding gardens, and at night, often suffer at the hands of abusive, drunken adults. It's no vacation. But for me, their "vacation" would give me three months to turn this place into something more habitable before they returned.

It took a long time and a lot of money. We painted the walls cheerful colors and divided the large ward-like rooms into smaller, homier bedrooms. And then I sent the water out for testing.

"Faulty test" was the message I got back. So, more carefully, we took the test again.

"Faulty test" was the second message. The third test revealed the same results. Finally, a scientist from the lab came and took the sample himself.

Two days later, the phone rang. "Mr. Cameron," he said, "I am sorry for all the messages that your tests were faulty. The fact was that I had never seen a water test come back so filthy. The water in that well is terribly contaminated with sewage."

My stomach turned. Those children I loved had been drinking sewer water for years!

That finding set us back until we could raise the money to dig new, deeper, safer wells.

I looked at Galina and Constantia and the other children, and I silently made them a promise: I'd be back. I'd be back, and I'd make sure those wells were dug. I'd be back, and I would make this place more like a home. They would see how much I loved and valued them as children, and then it would be easier for them to understand that Jesus loves them, too.

I was their dad.

CHAPTER

BE THEIR DAD

B E THEIR DAD." THE words rattled around in my brain as I tried to process what that meant on the way home.

Right away, I got to work raising the money and gathering the supplies needed to transform the orphanage over the summer. But I needed to do more than that; I also had several new children for whom to provide.

There was Ana, a petite little thing who made everyone around her laugh. She mimicked a thousand voices and had the perfect comic timing of a clown.

Of all the children, she was the only one I could really talk to from the first day. She had taught herself an amazing amount of English from the little bit of television the orphans were allowed to watch. (Most of the time, the workers had it on the news.)

When I asked about her past, though, her smiling face turned dark.

"There is a memory I have that never leaves me," she said. "It is there all the time. I was very little and was sleeping when I heard my father's angry voice. He was drunk and locked outside the house. He was pounding on the door with his fist, demanding that my mother come outside."

Finally, Ana's mother opened the door and went outside to her husband. Scared for her mother, Ana went to the window and saw that she was on the ground, her father beating her brutally.

"He kicked and kicked her until she stopped moving," she told me. "I ran out the back door and went to my neighbor's house. I begged them to come and stop my father from hurting my mother."

> Every child had a story that was worse than the last.

But the help was too late. Ana's mother was left handicapped for life from that beating. That one event resulted in Ana and her sister's being taken to the orphanage and her mom's giving in to the temptation of alcohol as a means of escaping the pain.

"I remember being so scared when she left me at the orphanage. I ran after my mother, but they grabbed me and brought me back. I wanted my mother, but no one cared."

Blinking back a tear, Ana continued, "When I dreamed, it was always of my mother. Then I would wake up and find myself still in the orphanage. Sometimes I still wonder how I can face another day without my mother."

Every child had a story that was worse than the last. With each one I heard, it was as if God was saying, "Philip, you think this place is bad, that living here is the worst thing that could happen to a child? Don't kid yourself. Their homes, their parents were far worse. The orphanage is better, but you know they need more. They need a dad, and you are it."

I knew what I had to do. From a construction point of view, this place was a much larger project than the orphanage where Stella lived—worse even than the orphanages in Romania. It would take hundreds of thousands of dollars and more faith and prayer than I was sure I was capable of.

In less than a year, we replaced every window, installed indoor toilets and showers, added a water purifier for the well, built a new roof, and cleaned the mold off the walls. We put in new beds, carpets, everything to make it into a real home. Making Chrissie and myself available to these children as their dad and mom was also a much larger project. Parenting required time—one-on-one, dependable, consistent time.

During all the years I had traveled to Romania and early on in Moldova, my work had centered on orphanages near cities large enough that I could stay nearby in a motel. It wasn't by design; it had just worked out that way.

But in Cupcui, I faced two issues. First, it was a three-hour round trip by car to the closest city where there were motels. And second, this calling to be Dad to these children meant I needed to be there. With my time divided now among my travels to minister and raise funds, my family in the States, and my work in Moldova, I needed to make as much as I could of each day in Moldova.

Most days, we started out on the trip at first light. But one day, we left the hotel later than usual so that we could swing through downtown. As we turned left to head out of town, we saw something we had never noticed before: the golden arches of McDonald's.

> To her, it was too precious to eat.

I stopped right in the middle of the intersection, cars honking and people behind me yelling at me in Romanian. I didn't care; I had an idea. Moments later, Vio and I stood in front of the shiny counter and spoke to the fresh-faced cashier.

"Tell her I want 100 hamburgers," I directed Vio.

"You want 100 hamburgers," he slowly said, making sure I meant what I'd said. "One hundred?"

Pulling my wallet out of my back pocket, I nodded. I knew the orphans had never heard of McDonald's or even eaten a hamburger.

This would be a great treat, regardless of the fact that the burgers would be stone cold by the time we got to the orphanage.

Two hours later, we entered the orphanage with six bags. At first, the kids weren't even sure what to do with the sandwiches, but they soon figured it out and wolfed them down and licked their fingers after they were finished.

All but one girl. She took her hamburger—wrapper and all—to her room. Hours later, I found her in her room still staring at it. To her, it was too precious to eat.

Shortly after that, Chrissie and I decided that the best thing to do was to buy a small house as close to the orphanage as possible so that we would have somewhere to stay during our visits. Most of the people in the village lived in hovels. Finding a house with flushing toilets, showers, working heat, and electricity was a challenge in itself.

Finally, we settled on a white stone cottage near the end of a dirt road just ten minutes from the orphanage. There was no well bringing running water, so we decided to build a well. It served as a means of water, not only for us, but also for the entire village.

Most of our neighbors were trying to survive by farming and had all manner of ducks and chickens in their yards. Our trip up the gravel road often was slowed behind a wooden wagon filled with produce, pulled by a horse that had seen better days. It was like going back in time.

We had forged a relationship with George, the orphanage director. By the time we were ready to open the home for visits from orphans, he agreed to let us bring eight or ten kids at a time over for the weekend. Galina, Constantia, and Ana were in the first group of eight to be our special guests. Except for the walk to school each day and "vacation" in the summer, these kids never left the orphanage. They had no concept of the outside world.

As we opened the door of our mission house, I tried to see it through their eyes. After entering the small mudroom, the first thing they saw was a closet filled with clean pajamas, socks, and slippers.

"Really? For us? We get to wear those?" they squealed with joy like kids at Christmas.

Chrissie was quick to nod and explain that the first thing we wanted them each to do was take a hot shower and change into these comfy, clean clothes.

Hot showers? One at a time? New clothes to wear? Wide-eyed, they took in every room of the house with raw and pure joy beyond anything I had ever seen. The house was filled with the smells of the dinner Chrissie was making. Good old fashioned spaghetti and meatballs was on the menu with green salad and fresh bread.

The kids joked with one another as they "fought" over who would shower first. Constantia came out on top, her eyes sparkling with delight, her dimple marking the depth of her smile. Ana was goofing around in the living room with the other kids, imitating the ducks in the yard, their schoolteacher, and, when she thought I wasn't listening, me.

Galina alone found her way to Chrissie's side, sweeping the floor that was already clean, wiping down the tables, doing anything she could think of to help. The others found blocks in a large red bucket in the corner of the living room and began to build a tower, giggling as if these were the most amazing toys on planet earth.

It was the first of many wonderful nights with the kids, the groups changing each weekend. Sometimes we'd go into the city for a special treat—a trip for pizza or shopping at the mall (yes, there is a mall, called "MallDova").

But from the very first night, we started a tradition that continues even to this day. After all the showers, the meal, the fun and games, we settled down in our pajamas.

"I have a movie I want you to watch with me," I told the girls. "It's called *Jesus*."

The kids were excited to see a movie, no matter the topic.

"Do you know who Jesus is?" I asked, looking up at their blank faces. "He is God, who came to earth as a man."

"Who is God?" one girl asked.

I started to explain, but stopped myself. "Let's watch together, then we can talk."

Campus Crusade for Christ and The Jesus Film Project translated this amazing movie, originally produced more than 20 years ago, into over a thousand languages. They took great care, using natives in the countries to recreate the dialogue into the language of people who had little ministry material available to them.

This was—and still is—an amazing tool to use to introduce Jesus to the orphans that is beyond my personal ability. I had spent hundreds of hours showing them the love of Christ through my actions, but they still didn't understand why I did it.

As we darkened the lights, the kids flopped down on the couches, piling on top of one another like a litter of kittens. After popping in the DVD, I sat down to join the girls. Chrissie had placed out bowls of popcorn, and I was amazed to see that as soon as the movie started, the girls ignored the buttery snack. The story on the television, the greatest story ever told, had their undivided attention.

> As she watched the Jesus movie, Galina said that God came to earth for her.

Years later, Galina told me, "I never really trusted you at first. I had many people come into my life and leave. The more I loved them, the more I hurt, so I decided not to love you and Mom or anyone."

She shared that with me, and though she was glad for the presents I brought and for making the orphanage so much better to live in, she didn't understand why I did it.

"It didn't make sense," she said. "We were nothing but orphans. Why leave your family to come and spend time with us? It was too good to be true, and I knew it would not last, so I kept my distance.

"You never talked about Jesus unless we asked. You would say, 'I love you this much [holding her hands about a foot apart], but Jesus loves you this much [holding her hands out as wide as she could].' But that made no sense to me. Who was Jesus? I never saw Him. If He was God, He certainly didn't care about me. I was an orphan. I didn't deserve anything. My own mother and father left me and never tried to find me. Jesus loved me? No way."

As she watched the Jesus movie, Galina said that God came to earth for her.

"He loved children. When they put Him on the cross, I began to weep and weep. I could not stop crying," she said. "My hard heart was not so hard. I asked Jesus into my heart that night, though I still understood so little."

It was very late when the movie was over, but the girls begged to watch it again. After pressing "play," I quickly fell asleep in my chair. The girls stayed awake to watch every word again. They could not get enough of it.

For the first time, Galina realized, "Jesus loves me! He sees me! He knows my name! He cares when I am hungry, alone, sick, scared. He is there and will never leave me. It was the greatest night of my life to discover this. Then your love became easier for me to understand. I went back to the orphanage after the weekend sad that our time was over and we had to go back to that terrible place, but my heart changed. I had hope."

The *Jesus* film soon brought up many questions for the children, and their questions became my invitation to tell them story after story from the Word of God.

Seeing Jesus come to life in the movie made my gospel messages to the children easier to grasp and gave them a deep desire to know more about God.

Those weekends were incredible times with the kids. One by one, they let down their guards like Galina did. We all grew closer—like a family. With every hour, I, Dad, grew, too, in my love and care for these incredible children with whom God had entrusted me.

We did everything we could to make the kids we couldn't bring to the mission house feel special, too. Chrissie and the kids would make massive trays of Jell-O—strawberry, lime, pineapple—and then carry them back to the orphanage. The kids had never seen Jell-O before, and their pleasure was intoxicating. I laughed until I hurt, watching them play with the "food."

We grew closer to these children than any with whom we had ever worked. Chrissie and I came to see them as our children in a way that I cannot describe. When we were in America, we could not wait to get back. When we were in Moldova, we could not wait to raise more money and make life easier for "our kids."

I made a point to communicate with these kids without learning Romanian. I knew that if they saw how much I cared, they would want to talk to me, and it would give them a reason to learn English—a life skill that would give them an advantage.

I spent hours and hours with each of them, teaching one word at a time. "Book." "Glasses." "Cookie." "Hair." Then a big one: "Grade."

Each of the kids quickly learned to get his or her report card ready for me when I was there. I wanted to have a connection with each of them so that they knew someone cared if they passed or failed, studied or slacked off.

It became a standing joke:

10 = Awesome
9 = Good
8 = Okay, not great
7 = Trouble
6 = Pow! (I would mock a whack with my fist.)

We'd all laugh, but there was a serious undertone to all the joking. Someone had to encourage these children to focus on their studies, or they'd never have a chance in life. The orphanage workers had no use for encouragement; their teachers didn't care.

In my heart, I was Dad, and keeping the children focused on their grades was a very important part of the job.

As the kids lined up over and over and the months went by, I started to see improvement. Just as I cared about their grades, they began to care as well. It warmed my heart to see the extra effort they were investing.

One day we were in the lobby talking, and one of the older girls, Marina, motioned us upstairs where several of the girls were standing, talking, and giggling. Pointing us to the chairs in the middle of the room, they asked Chrissie and me to sit.

> I am rarely speechless, but in that moment, I was at a complete loss for words.

"What do your kids call you?" one of them asked.

"Well, they call me Dad."

"And Chrissie, what do they call her?"

"They call her Mom."

Immediately, the girls started chatting among themselves in Romanian. Finally, Marina piped up, "Can we call you Mom and Dad?"

I am rarely speechless, but in that moment, I was at a complete loss for words. You see, I'd never told the kids what God had spoken to me. I'd been doing everything in my power to be their dad, but I'd never said the word.

Never in my life have I felt as I did in that moment. A year had passed since the Lord said, "Be their dad." Now the kids were asking me the same thing.

I was, and am, their dad.

CHAPTER

THE VALLEY OF THE SHADOW OF DEATH

S EPTEMBER IN SOUTHERN ALABAMA always comes as a welcome relief from the scorching summer sun. The heat becomes more manageable. The kids are back in school. There is more order to life than the chaos of summer with four kids.

I was running late that day in 2002, more than a year before finding Cupcui, keenly aware that Chrissie would have food ready to put on the table before I could possibly get there. I hated to be late. The kids were planning to attend youth group at church

> "You have to come," my mother's voice came across the line before the word was even out of my mouth. "

that evening, so family time would be limited to a quick meal, followed by taking turns chauffeuring the kids around town. I walked in the door to find Chrissie running behind as well, a rare thing.

With a few minutes to spare, I sat down in my chair and turned on the television. The phone beside me rang. As the sound filled the room, I suddenly flashed back to the day my dad had called me 22 years ago. And just as that phone call had changed the course of my life, so did this one.

"Hel—"

"You have to come," my mother's voice came across the line before the word was even out of my mouth. "You have to come now. Your dad is very sick. I just left him at the hospital. He is having trouble with his heart. Can you come tomorrow?"

My mother has never been one to overreact about anything. Calm was her middle name. And she never asks for anything. I knew if she was asking me to come, it was serious.

I spoke to her for only a few minutes, checking my watch and assuring her I would be on the next flight, knowing I could catch a red-eye to Scotland if I hurried. Within minutes of hanging up with my mother, I called Lisa Crews and told her to book the flight.

I grabbed the first clothes I saw and stuffed them into my well-traveled suitcase. I kissed Chrissie and the kids, rushed out to the car, and put it in gear. I was only a few miles from the house when my cell phone rang. It was Lisa.

"Philip, I just got off the phone with your brother in Scotland," she said. "It's not as bad as your mom seemed to think. Your dad will be fine. He'll be in the hospital for a few days, but you don't need to rush over there tonight. Really."

Her words tempted me. It would be so easy to cancel the flight, turn my car around, and go home to a nice meal. I'd been on the road so much lately, and I really wanted time at home with my family, but I felt a stirring in my spirit telling me not to turn around.

"No, I need to go now," I said to Lisa. "Thanks for checking, but I really need to go now. I'll call you tomorrow."

It was morning when I landed in Scotland, and the crisp fall air woke me up as I walked out of the airport with my mom. She looked tired and fragile, nothing like the strong woman I was used to seeing.

She and my dad were more than husband and wife—they really were soul mates. They finished each other's sentences. They completed each other. I could not imagine her without him, or him without her.

Slowly walking to the car, she leaned into my shoulder as I put my arm around her. Words weren't needed. Together we prayed without saying a word.

The hospital in Aberdeen is a modern facility on the far end of town. I walked into the building, and the smells of disinfectant and medicine washed over me. The hospital was for sick people, and my dad was always the strongest person I knew—a powerhouse. What was he doing in this place? I had to admit to myself, he had never been quite the same since his surgery to remove the cancer from his back years ago, but still, this was Dad. He had to be okay.

I found his room on the third floor, right across from a noisy nurses' station. Without knocking, I walked in, and he looked at me with surprise.

"What are you doing here? Am I sicker than anyone told me?" he asked. I assured him he would be fine.

"Well, then, I hope you got a cheap ticket over here," he countered.

"Well, as a matter of fact, the ticket cost me $1,000," I bantered back.

"I am worth it," he said with a hint of his famous smile.

I smiled back. On the inside, I was anything but smiling. He was swollen with fluid, his skin was a sick shade of yellow, and the pain was visible on his face. His kidneys were failing, and it caused his back to ache until it was almost unbearable. Still he kept at me.

"So what are the plans? When are you going back to Moldova? What is the news? What are you doing right now for Jesus?" Dad asked.

I found a chair and pulled up close to his bed. He knew every project and every child almost as well as I did. Although he was only able to make a few trips, he was forever on the phone with me, walking me through each situation, helping with challenges, poking holes in my strategies. And he loved the children. He loved to hear about our time with them, how their health improved, the joy we were starting to find in their hearts.

As I detailed the latest events, he'd respond, "Aye. Aye. That's good, boy. Aye."

But each word pained him.

When I finished my report, I excused myself and stepped out to the nurses' station.

"Do you know when the doctor may be around?" I asked the nurse at the desk. "I'd like to talk to him."

Nodding, she pointed down the hall to the left. There he stood, looking over a chart, a young man in his early thirties. I walked over at once.

"Doctor, I am Simon Cameron's son, Philip. I am very worried about him; I have never seen him like this. His kidneys don't seem to be working at all, he's full of fluid, and the pain is almost unbearable. Could you hook him up to a dialysis machine overnight, give the kidneys a break, and take some of the fluid pressure off his heart? It would help."

> Universal health care had stolen the decisions about care from the hands of the Scottish doctors, and they stopped fighting it years ago.

He stopped me cold. "You are kidding, right? Your dad is 71. We don't have the money to be spending on giving him dialysis," he said, shaking his head and walking off without another word.

Universal health care had stolen the decisions about care from the hands of the Scottish doctors, and they stopped fighting it years ago. Now, it was all about money, return on investment. Perhaps for a younger man, they would do the treatment, but a 71-year-old? Forget it.

I chased the man down the hall, barely catching him at the elevator.

"But Doctor, you don't understand. That is a very important man in that room," I said, pointing down the hall. "He is known all over the world as an evangelist, he has a Bible college, he has helped orphans all over Eastern Europe...."

Before I could finish, he cut me off. "I am sorry," he said, the apology ringing hollow and false in my ears. He stepped in the elevator and pushed the button, and the conversation was over.

When I returned to the room, Dad's eyes were closed. Mom was holding his hand. Aside from the creaking sound the door made as it closed, the room was quiet. After a moment, Dad opened his eyes and looked at me.

"Son, I need you to pray for me. Pray for your dad."

I nodded my head and stood there awkwardly. Even as I write these words, I look back on that moment with regret. Did he mean "pray with me," as in the prayers that he knows I do all day, or did he mean he wanted me to lay hands on him and pray aloud for him right then and there?

I wish I could say I prayed out loud for him in that sterile hospital room, but all I could do was put my arm around my mom and wait until he drifted off into a fitful sleep. It was late; we stayed all day at the hospital after I had flown all night. I was tired to the bone and ready for bed.

That night I slept soundly, never turning over until the first hint of sun peeked through the curtains. I quickly awoke, cleaned up, and got ready to return to the hospital.

But it was too late. He died at 1:00 in the morning. It was September 11, 2002.

An hour later, we were gathered around his hospital bed, my mom, my sister, my brother, and a handful of cousins. It was surreal. How could this man who had been the foundation of my life be gone? He was the only man whose approval I had ever needed. Gone. How would I know what to do next? If I was doing it right? I felt as helpless as a child.

The next few days were a blur. Dad, in his three-piece suit, was in his coffin in the living room, as is the tradition in Scotland. Relatives came from all over, as did preachers, former students, and friends. I remember none of their words of condolence.

> I knew what he would be saying to me if he was still with us: "What are you doing today, my boy? What are you doing for Jesus?"

As my brother and I carried him out to be buried, they played a recording I made of him years ago: "Yea, though I walk through the valley of the shadow of death, I will fear no evil, for Thou art with me…" (Psalm 23:4, KJV).

Once his body was lowered into the ground, my spirit began to stir. I knew what I had to do. I knew what he would be saying to me if he was still with us: "What are you doing today, my boy? What are you doing for Jesus?"

I turned my grief into action, making plans, even as I was still in Scotland, to continue our efforts in Moldova. By the time the winter of 2003 rolled around, I was anxious to see Stella and the others. There was much to do, and I knew, beyond a shadow of a doubt, that Simon was now watching, praying for me when we found Cupcui that winter.

More and more over the next year, Cupcui became the focal point of my trips to Moldova, the needs of the children there more pressing. But on the way, we always stopped by Hincesti to see Stella and the others; Vio was always by my side.

Often, Stella was sick in bed, but she always had a smile for me. I would bring her more sewing needles, cloth, and threads. I also brought her little bottles of perfume because she loved the fragrance so much.

As we pulled up, I remember commenting to Vio how different even the outside of the building looked. It was nothing like the "dying rooms" I first encountered seven or so years ago. I was happy for Stella and the others.

We pulled up, and the kids ran to the windows to see who was there.

"Philip! Philip!" they called, their accents thick (making my name sound more like "Phiiiilip"), rushing into my arms as they had before. I had watched these children grow up, knew almost all of them by name.

But I instantly knew something wasn't right.

Where is Stella? I thought as I looked around. Unless she was sick, she was always the first to greet me. We got to work unloading the gifts, but my mind was on her. Was she okay? As soon as I placed the gifts into the anxious hands of all the kids, I went to check her room.

Before I could get down the hall, Dr. Liudmila—the orphanage doctor, a short, round woman of few words and even fewer smiles—greeted me with a firm handshake, thanking us for the gifts we were unloading. I cut her short.

> Stella had been moved to a different facility because she was too old for this one.

"Where is Stella?" I asked.

Dr. Liudmila looked at Vio and then back at me with a shake of her head. I turned to Vio.

"Make sure she understands what I am asking," I said. "Where is Stella?"

At once the two of them began a long exchange in Romanian. I had been to the area enough times that I could usually pick out a few words of any conversation, but I was completely lost. I had no idea what they were saying.

But one look at Vio's face was enough for me to know that the news was not good. Finally, he started to translate. Stella had been moved to a different facility because she was too old for this one.

I felt the color drain from my face. How could they just move her? This place was finally livable—unlike the other orphanages in Moldova. It was the only home Stella knew, the only family she really had.

The story got worse.

"At the other orphanage, the workers mistreated her. Dr. Liudmila doesn't have all the details, but Stella ran away from the orphanage," Vio told me in broken English. "That's how bad it was. She is gone."

Hearing all of this, I was angry. After all the work I had done there, the dozens of visits over the years, I thought someone would have

143

contacted me. The director knew how important Stella was to me. Yet she just stood there as though she had just shared something as trivial as a weather report.

I tried to smile at the children while we finished delivering the gifts, but I was hurting. I was frightened for Stella—and so angry that it was hard to focus. As soon as we could manage, Vio and I were back on the road.

It was at times like these that I was especially glad to have Vio in my life. He had connections with Moldovan government leaders, the military, and the police. I was confident that he would find some answers about this dear girl for me; there weren't that many orphanages, and the country was not that large.

What Vio learned weeks later frightened me to the core. By several reports, she was in Transnistria, a disputed area whose people did not consider themselves part of Moldova. No bigger than the size of a United States county, the region was known for its violence and was controlled by the Russian mafia. It was a dark, unruly place with a border that deterred the few people brave enough to want to go in. Murders, rapes, robberies go unnoticed, unexplored. The Embassy has firm warnings urging Americans not to go there; it knows not even Moldovan police will enter to help if someone is in trouble.

In spite of the risks, Vio made several trips there over the next few months and spoke to many people who claimed to have seen Stella. She was working as a prostitute.

I heard these words as a Christian pastor with no judgment. I know the heart and life of an orphan like Stella in Moldova. These children are raised in a world where no decision is their own. From day one in the orphanage, they are told, "This is your bed. This is your shirt, your jeans. Eat this. Go to bed now. Today it is your turn to take a shower."

You've read how cruel and cold the orphanage workers are; children are beaten often with no cause. At school, they are made fun of and told that they are less than nothing, and therefore deserve nothing because they are orphans.

What are they supposed to do on the outside? They are not educated beyond the ninth grade and lack the skills necessary to even boil an egg.

And it was worse for Stella. With her handicaps and her seizures, I could only imagine her life in the days and weeks after she ran away from the orphanage. Did she sleep outside, get food from garbage cans, and beg on the streets?

> "Stella is dead," said Dr. Liudmila. "HIV."

Did she trust the wrong person and end up walking the streets? Was she beaten, abused?

Or was selling her body the only way she could afford to buy food and avoid starvation? Did she feel that since she was "nothing," it wouldn't matter? After all, she was "just an orphan."

I pressed Vio to keep looking. I wanted to find her, rescue her. We'd find a place for her to stay. Every trip back I would ask for a report as soon as I saw Vio or when I visited Hincesti.

Then I heard the words that caused me to weep.

"Stella is dead," said Dr. Liudmila. "HIV."

Chrissie was standing beside me, and I felt the room move under my feet. I thought of what that poor girl's last days must have been like. Used by monsters until they killed her. Was anyone there to comfort her in the last stages of her illness? Did anyone hold her hand, look into her eyes, and let her know that he cared?

She had no family. No friends. My tears started to fall faster, and I wiped them away with the sleeve of my jacket. Without another word, I walked out of the room.

I knew Stella was with Jesus; we had talked about Him many times. But why did she have to die that way? I begged the Lord for answers. It was not fair.

Losing her opened my eyes even more to the future that awaited the other orphan girls I loved so much. I knew that the June after they turn 16, orphans are sent away, but where would they go? Would they all turn out like Stella?

They couldn't go home to their families; of that I was certain. Obviously, if they had family members who loved them and could care for them, they would not be at the orphanage in the first place.

On my next visit to Cupcui, I started asking the older girls what their plans were after they aged out of the orphanage, how they would survive. They all said the same thing: "I want to get a job working in a kitchen."

That puzzled me. Why a job in a kitchen? Is that really the best they could hope for?

"In a kitchen," Constantia explained to me, "there is always food, and it is warm. I can sleep outside at night. And if I have one meal a day, I can live."

My children in Montgomery were raised to believe they could be anything they put their minds to. Doctors, lawyers, preachers, engineers—they could do it if they did the work. They had a future.

These kids had no concept whatsoever of a future beyond the basics to survive. A job in a kitchen was the very best they could hope for, dream of.

What these girls didn't know was that the unemployment rate was 70 percent in this part of the country. There were no kitchen jobs. Their ninth-grade educations would not qualify them for anything, and as scorned orphans, they would be the last to be considered for any position, even if there was an opening.

So what would happen to them? What had already happened to the girls who had aged out last year and the year before?

I started asking the directors, the government officials, and I began reading articles online about what happens. It seemed that the government had decided that it was only obligated to care for orphans until they turn sixteen, so that was the law of the land. The June after every orphan's sixteenth birthday, the teenagers are given $30 and a bus ticket back to the village from which they came.

So a girl like Constantia or Galina would be given a bus ticket to Chisinau, a two-hour bus trip to the capital city, and then she would take another bus to the village from which she had come on the other side of the country.

She would travel alone, with all that she owned in a plastic bag or cardboard box, terrified, not knowing how to survive beyond that kitchen job fantasy.

With just a few clicks of the mouse, I learned about this routine. It is as well-documented as any policy, and, believe me, the sex traffickers know it, too. It just makes sense. Moldova is known as the engine of the sex trafficking machine, and no one is more vulnerable than a 16-year-old beautiful orphan girl.

> I learned that more than four hundred thousand women and girls had simply vanished from Moldova.

To make matters worse, the workers in the orphanage often will tip off the traffickers with a call that alerts them, "I just put four Olympic-quality girls on the bus to Chisinau." For that, they will be rewarded more than a month's pay.

I learned that more than 400,000 women and girls had simply vanished from Moldova. Some were kidnapped. Others were lured by stories of fake jobs in foreign countries. As soon as they were in a trafficker's care, all hope was lost. I was told they would be out of the country and sold for as little as $3,500.

They would be drugged and beaten until they submitted to being used 30 to 50 times a day, making $350,000 a year for the trafficker. It was easy money for him. It was safer than selling drugs, easier than selling drugs. A little girl, once she is beaten, won't fight back.

Some officials have told me that less than one percent of these girls ever escape, and even if they do, they are emotionally damaged for life. How does someone ever heal from that?

All of a sudden, I looked at the girls at Cupcui differently. I was their dad. I had to do something, or they could wind up just like my Stella!

Then I had an idea that could have come only from God: We will build a house for the girls who are aging out and have it ready by June. We will feed them, we will allow them to finish school, we will protect them, and we will show them the love of Jesus every single day.

And we will make sure the devil regrets what he did to Stella because we will call this home, this place of refuge, Stella's House!

CHAPTER 16

STELLA'S HOUSE

A S THIS GOES TO press, combating sex trafficking is the cause du jour, and I agree that it should be—not just today, but for a long time.

But the majority of high-profile ministries and nonprofits are spending most of their money on raising awareness (whatever that means), on rescuing (though less than one percent of the girls who are rescued stay out of prostitution—out of options or so broken that they return to this terrible life), and on short rehab programs by people with good intentions.

Here is the problem I faced. I am a father, not just to my four kids, but to the dozens of girls I was raising who were living in this orphanage. I was suddenly aware that Ana, Constantia, Galina, and the 65 other orphans practically had targets drawn on their backs. But what was I going to do about it? How could I protect them from this nightmare?

They needed a place to go, a real home in which to live. They needed to finish their education, literally grow up and learn to live and function as members of a family.

I needed to open a home—a big one—but I had no clue how to do it, and I didn't have the money to make it happen.

Frankly, the younger orphans are, the easier it is to raise money to help them. Raising money for abandoned and abused puppies and kittens is easier, too, but we won't go there. It's almost impossible to raise money to help teenagers; countless other nonprofits and ministries have tried, but the assumption is that teens are old enough to take care of themselves.

> I prayed. I sought counsel. I asked people in Moldova whom I trusted. Finally, I came up with a plan.

If only that were true.

So Stella's House was born in 2006—not to be an answer for those who have been trafficked (though we have taken in several who were), but primarily to offer girls a place to stay when they age out of the orphanage, safe from the threat of sex traffickers.

I prayed. I sought counsel. I asked people in Moldova whom I trusted. Finally, I came up with a plan.

We would open a home for these girls in the city, allowing them to finish high school and then go on to vocational school or college. Chrissie and I would come and spend as much Mom and Dad time as we could, but we'd also hire a houseparent/missionary to be there twenty-four seven. The girls would do chores, like cooking and cleaning, skills they needed for a lifetime, and that would reduce our operational costs.

All I needed to do was clear the plan with the government.

You would think that a plan and proposal for a nonprofit to open a home to protect aged-out 16-year-old orphans from sex traffickers would be met with cheers of joy from these cash-strapped officials.

"Mr. Cameron, what are you thinking?" a frightening-looking woman with badly dyed red hair and an ugly beige suit asked me. "They are just orphans, nobodies. We have fed them, educated them, put a roof over their heads. Why do you care? It is their time to become useful members of society now. We have other pressing needs. Real issues. Don't make this a problem for us."

Like with any dad, that answer was not good enough for me. I kept trying other agencies, other towns, other levels of government.

"I know your type; don't think I don't," a portly official said as he pointed his sausage-like finger at me. A strange look crossed his face, and he leaned back in his chair. A leer perhaps?

"You must have a market for these girls yourself. What is your plan? Sell these girls on the street, keep the money for yourself? Or maybe you plan to sell their hearts, kidneys, whatever organs you selfish Americans need. Leave me alone," he said, dismissing me with a wave of his hand.

His ugly words just made me more determined. Soon, I became like the woman in the Bible with the unjust judge. I would not leave this alone. I would not take no for an answer. I had to protect my girls.

Finally, I was sitting in the well-appointed office of the governor of the area. Two young assistants were busy bringing us cookies and strong, bitter coffee.

He had granted me audience because I had given so much food and coal to the local orphanages. I had solved a problem for him. He didn't care about the children, but as long as I was helping with the orphans, it meant he had fewer issues with which to deal.

I sat in front of him, knowing how hard the hearts of these officials are. Children are of no value to them, and orphaned children mean even less.

Still, I tried to appeal to him from one father to another. Surely he knew as well as I did the nightmare that each one of these girls would face. He was unmoved.

I kept talking, and Vio kept translating. I tried to look sincere and nonthreatening. In the simplest of terms, Vio was helping tell him what we would offer the girls—food, clothes, an education, life skills.

"Education?" he stopped Vio mid-sentence. "Education?"

It seemed I had landed on the one thing Communists are big on providing.

Vio was quick to say, "Da! Da!" Yes, we would guarantee to keep these girls in school. So we struck a deal that I could take the girls in as long as they were in school while they were in my care. Some would be still in high school, some would be in vocational tech training, while others would be going to university. But they had my word that every girl would remain in school.

The plan started to come together. If the girls lived in the city, it meant that there was public transportation to take them to school. That was vital because the girls all would be on different schedules and in dozens of schools and colleges scattered about Chisinau. Transporting them in our own vans was not an option.

We started looking for an appropriate house and were floored by the price of real estate! Our needs were very specific; I wanted a house large enough for the 20 girls who would age out of Cupcui in just a few weeks. We had no time to lose, but it had to be in a safe area where we could provide good security.

The process of building in Moldova was different from anything I had ever encountered. The country had no banking system, and no one could take out a mortgage to buy a home. Instead, people bought land and, as they had the money, would build homes in stages.

All over town there are shells of houses made of stone and cement—nothing but the basement, floors, and partial walls. Sometimes there are roofs. The shells are left like this for years and even decades until the family has the money to build more or decides to sell.

We looked at countless shells all over the city before we turned onto a street called Str. Speranta. In English, it would be called Hope Street. I knew immediately we had found the right place.

Garth Coonce, a great giant of faith, was with me on that trip. He had been my friend for many years. The founder of TCT Ministries,

Garth had brought 24-hour Christian television to many towns that had never had easy access to the gospel on television.

Garth is a dear, dear friend and a brilliant businessman. Seeing this shell, knowing the need, he gave us $100,000 to get started on the project as soon as we walked the site. He knew in his spirit that it was right for us, just as I did.

His gift was the miracle—and the encouragement—I needed to pull out all the stops to make this a reality.

> His gift was the miracle—and the encouragement—I needed to pull out all the stops to make this a reality.

As the construction and decorating neared completion, I drove out to Cupcui to meet with the girls.

Ten of the girls and I squeezed into one of the rooms. I had the only chair in the place, while the girls sat on the beds or on the vinyl floor.

"I bought a house," I told them. "For you, for when you age out of here. Every one of you is smart enough to be anything you want to be—a doctor, a teacher—anything. But you need an education, and you need to finish growing up. I want to help you do that.

"I will take you there to see it soon, but for now, you need to keep up your grades, think about what you want to study, and trust me. Mom and I will take care of you."

I looked at their faces—their emotions ranging from joy to boredom to disbelief. It didn't matter. For now, all I really needed was for each of them to stay put, not leave while I finished the building. I'd come too far to lose any of them now.

In June, when the girls of Cupcui aged out, Stella's House was still not ready, but was close to completion. Thankfully, we were able to house the girls in the mission house near Cupcui until the construction was complete. During that time they would commute an hour and a half to school each day.

By November, we brought them from the orphanage and welcomed them to the only real home they had ever known. My daughter, Melody, decorated and appointed it as nice as my home in Montgomery. These girls were no longer orphans; they were my children, so why would I give them anything less?

One of the most joyful days of my life was the day I gave those first girls a tour of what would be their new home. I watched with tears in my eyes as they discovered a thousand things that made this place a home—not a warehouse for children, like they were used to. Everything was clean, and small trinkets and pictures on the walls gave each room character.

There were no more than three girls to a room, giving them the space and privacy that they had never had. The beds were made with matching brightly colored comforters, soft pillows, firm mattresses, things they had never seen in their lives. They even had drawers and closets—furnishings they had never needed because they owned nothing.

> Like in any home, we had rules.

But what really got their attention was the kitchen. There was no lock on the door. They were allowed in at any time. They could make a sandwich or snack any time of the day. They could choose what food to eat and when to eat. These were all unheard of concepts at the orphanage!

"When I first walked into Stella's House, I thought I was dreaming," Galina said of her first time at Stella's House. "It was the most amazing thing. I never had to share my bed with anybody or wake up in the middle of the night to move my bed because of the leaking problems we had at our orphanage before Dad fixed it."

The girls moved in. The home soon was filled with giggles and tears and all the craziness a gaggle of girls can offer. I hired Nina and Anatol Pislaru, a former assistant director at Cupcui and his wife, to be house-parents. Vio kept a watchful eye between my visits.

I shared my faith when asked, but I did not force any of the girls to go to church or read the Bible. I was purposeful in not putting a television in Stella's House, bringing one out only on special occasions. The *Jesus* film was one of several movie options, along with other carefully selected films.

Like in any home, we had rules. They had to stay in school (and do well), they had to share chores with the others, they could not date (lest they disappear forever), and they had to learn to function as a family.

The girls had homework and chores. For their fun, I wanted them interacting with one another, playing games, sharing their days, being a family.

When one of the new girls asked why I did this for them—and they all asked—I answered, "Because of all God has done for me." Their questions allowed me to share my faith at their pace. When they asked for a Bible, I was ready with one. When they wanted to visit a church, I had the van ready to take them.

I watched these girls transform, both spiritually and emotionally—some almost overnight, some more slowly. When you are raised as an orphan, you hold everything you are given close to you—willing to fight because of the fear of losing what precious little you own.

They slowly began to let down their guards. Over time, they began to relax in the knowledge that the clothes they were given were really theirs. No one would beat them or yell at them. They had been orphans together; now they were sisters.

They learned to share. They learned to trust. They learned what it was to be loved unconditionally. And with that, one at a time, they asked Jesus to be their Lord and Savior.

I never told them to start Bible studies, but they did. I never told them to pray together, to share their scars, their dreams, their lives with one another, but they did. Never in my life have I seen any group of kids turn a vague concept of God into such a deep, abiding relationship with Jesus Christ. It took my breath away!

My visits to Moldova were now split between the orphans still in Cupcui and the girls at Stella's House. The orphanage was in decent shape and was filled with more kids than ever. I loved going there, seeing how the kids had changed and grown since the last visit, checking their report cards, bringing small gifts.

Early on, I learned that these kids never complain. If they are sick with the flu, or even something much more serious, they keep it to themselves. The workers at the orphanage had trained and conditioned them that no one cares if they are sick or hurting. No one comes if you are crying at night. There were no trips to doctors, no over-the-counter medications to ease symptoms; if you were sick, too bad.

But Galina had concerned me for some time, and her problem with her eyes was getting worse and worse. Her vision was darkening, her headaches were more acute, and her dizzy spells seemed to come out of nowhere.

In Moldova, there is so-called universal health care, but orphans are in their own lowly class. I finally found a private doctor who would see her. After a battery of tests, he confirmed that she had a benign brain tumor that was pressing on the nerve behind her eye. It was inoperable and progressive. He could give her pain pills, but suggested that she drink a lot of wine instead.

Galina was crestfallen. In the hallway, I gave her a hug and assured her this was not the end of the story. Like any dad, I was going to do whatever I could to see my little girl healed.

"Next stop," I told her, "will be the Embassy. We will get you a visa, and I will find a doctor in America who will operate on you and get that tumor gone. I promise. Start praying for favor at the Embassy and the right doctor to step forward to help you."

We brought Galina over to the States on a medical visa. The first thing a doctor did was give her an eye test and fit her with a pair of glasses. Instantly, the girl could see. I was so happy for her, but remembered all the tears she had shed struggling to do homework when she could not see the blackboard at school. All those wasted years, all because an orphan was not worth taking to an eye doctor!

Next we saw a surgeon who confirmed and documented the exact size and position of the tumor. Yes, it was progressive, but he could remove it. He had operated on much more complex ones than this, and he waived his fee. He gave her medication that would help her symptoms and pain and explained the need to wait a few months to do the surgery, but said that in less than a year, if all went well, she would be healed.

Galina didn't know what to say. She had hardly gotten used to the fact that she could see with glasses. Now there was hope, a plan, for the headaches to be taken care of. No more dizziness? No more struggling to get through each day? It was almost more than she could bear.

"I was very nervous about the surgery," Galina later recalled. "I was very nervous that something could go wrong, that I could end up paralyzed."

Although I was happy and smiling on the outside, I have to confess that I was worried, too. Brain surgery. The thought of them putting my little girl to sleep and drilling into her brain was a frightening thought. Yes, I knew doctors performed surgeries all the time, but this was my girl! It was different.

I left her with Chrissie and the other four kids at home and continued the work as we waited for the surgery.

At the same time, I had started a construction project at another home called Straseni, which housed 700 children, just a short drive from Stella's House. While I didn't physically have the time to invest in getting to know all the children as well as I had come to know the kids at Cupcui, when I discovered the place, saw how terrible the windows were, knowing winter was coming, I had to act.

Turning to the director, I asked, "How many windows do you need?"

"I think 100," he said. He looked at his shoes. "Maybe 200." Another pause. "Perhaps 300."

In all, it took 391 windows to protect the 700 children in this orphanage from the danger of freezing to death.

While we were at the Straseni Orphanage to check on the windows, I met a young girl named Irina, whose story I learned later. Her dad was a drunk, but her mother was kind, a hard worker, and always made sure there was food for her children and warm clothes.

But when Irina was five, her world turned upside down. Her mother became sick with pulmonary edema—fluid in her lungs. Within three months of going to the hospital, she died.

Her father had no interest in or concern for the four little ones who were left behind. He would go into long drunken binges and beat the children. They would hide under the bed they shared, hoping he would not find them. He always did.

The family spiraled into poverty, there was never enough food to eat, and their clothes became dirty and shabby.

Once she told me, "The kids at school who used to be our friends made fun of us. They called us names and made up mean songs about the poor children. I hated going to school, and I hated going home. Nowhere was safe."

Irina was relieved when she was taken away from her father and placed in Straseni, in spite of its terrible conditions. There was at least food, she told me, even if it sometimes had worms in it.

She was six years old, had survived the hell of her father, and decided that as bad as the orphanage was, she would be okay. There were kids to play with, and she was far away from her raging father.

But three months later, her uncle removed her from the orphanage. Once again, Irina found herself in another kind of living hell. Her uncle had taken her for one reason alone: so she could work like a slave on his farm.

The family made it clear that she was not one of them, she was an orphan, and she should be grateful for the scraps of food she was given. She had to get up before dawn to milk cows, feed chickens, and care for the horses.

She would go to school, and the moment she was home, she had to shuck corn, shell peas, weed the garden, and complete countless other tasks too big for a six year-old. There was no time for her to do homework, and her grades got worse and worse. At school, the teachers yelled at her, and at home, her aunt and uncle beat her.

Still, it was the only family she had, and she tried to please her uncle, failing on all counts.

When she was seven, she took her uncle's lunch to him at the building where he worked as a security guard. As she handed him his food, he grabbed her and started to tickle her.

Irina laughed as he tickled her, her little heart soaring with pleasure. He must really like her! She had pleased him that day!

And then his hand moved. What had started as a tickle turned into a sexual assault. Irina tried to pull away, but he kept groping her. She started to scream, but he covered her mouth with his huge hand.

Then a door slammed, and she heard the voice of her aunt. She had walked in and seen what had happened; she was furious!

At Irina! A seven-year-old!

Within days she was back at Straseni, to the wet beds and moldy walls. Here is the one thing she told me that caused me not to forget her: "All the time at my uncle's house and then in the orphanage, at night I would pray. I didn't know God," she said. "I didn't know to Whom I was praying, but I begged God for someone to love me, to care if I lived or died. I wanted to be hugged. I wanted to know I was special to someone."

On a sunny June afternoon in 2008, Chrissie and I dropped by to see how the installation of the windows had gone, to make sure everything was in order. The director gave me a tour, pleased to show me the progress.

As we wandered back to his office, I saw 18 teenage girls lined up on a blue bench in front of the administration building. Every one of them was dressed in ratty jeans and a tee shirt and spotted with pale green paint.

He waved his arm at them, "They all must go," he told me. "All of them turned 16 this year. Yesterday was the last day of school. They just finished painting their rooms for the new kids we will soon take in."

Horror washed over me. Eighteen Stellas. Eighteen Constantias. Eighteen Galinas. Eighteen Anas. Eighteen prime targets for sex traffickers. Eighteen girls with no place to go. I couldn't look away from their innocent faces. I knew what awaited them; they had no clue. It was like seeing a child running after a ball into the street and into an oncoming car that until then had gone unseen. I had to stop this nightmare, but how?

I turned to my wife and said, "Chrissie, that room at Stella's that is set up for study, if we removed the desks and put in beds, how many girls could we take?"

She was quiet for a moment as she turned the idea over in her mind. "I think three is the most we could take."

I looked at the faces before me. Innocent. Beautiful. Alone. How could I pick three? What would happen to the other 15? My heart cried to the Lord. This was so unfair. How could I pick three and condemn the others to hell on earth?

It was impossible. I told the director not to send them away yet, that we would be back the next day. At 8:00 the following morning, I was back as promised, but with some of the girls from Stella's House. I made them choose.

"Talk to the girls. Find out who is willing to work hard to have a future, which of these girls is willing to live by the rules and live at Stella's House. You have to pick just three more sisters."

And they did.

THREE WE SAVED

I DON'T KNOW HOW THE girls managed to choose three of the eighteen girls on that bench, but they did. They took the decision very seriously, welcoming in three girls who were willing and able to work hard for a successful future. Every day I think about the girls whom I was forced to turn away. Every day my heart is burdened by that horrible day.

But I have been so blessed by the three girls who joined our family that day.

Natalie, for instance, is one of those girls who light up a room when they walk in.

> Natalie, for instance, is one of those girls who light up a room when they walk in.

Her story came pouring out a few days after her arrival. When she was four years old, her mother was in a tragic accident. She became very sick and lost her vision. Natalie's earliest memory was fearing her mother would never get out of bed, that she would die and leave her all alone.

Her grandmother came and took the little girl to live with her, but she was desperately poor, and there was never food to eat.

"Sometimes we would go into the woods behind her house and look for mushrooms, hoping to find a few bites of anything we could eat," Natalie told me. "At night we shared the same small bed. She loved me, but she was too poor to care for me."

When Natalie was seven years old, her grandmother took her on a long bus ride to the orphanage more than an hour away.

"She didn't tell me where we were going," Natalie said. "I knew I was at the age when I needed to go to school, and when I saw all of the kids, I thought that was where we were. But it still didn't make sense. How could I go to school so far from home?"

Standing there in front of the orphanage, Natalie learned the truth.

"You'll be safe here. You'll have your own bed, and there will always be something to eat," her grandmother promised her. "Your mom and I can visit you."

The only thing that took a bit of the sting from being abandoned at the orphanage was that her uncle (her mother's youngest brother) was there. Nicolai was older and would look out for her.

But Natalie was so very sad. "I had not seen my mother in the three years since I went to live with my grandmother. I was afraid I would forget what her face looked like. In all the time I was at Grandmother's, she had never visited me, and that was only a short walk away. How was I to believe she would ever visit me here?"

Nicolai began to show her how to survive in the orphanage, how to wash her clothes, which workers would be nice, which ones to avoid.

"I don't know how I would have survived without him," Natalie told me. "He would come and encourage me to study hard and get good grades so we would have a chance to survive. He made me feel not quite so alone, but I needed my mom. I was a girl, and every girl has questions. I have never known who my dad is, never seen him. Why? Would I ever know the truth?"

The weed-infested grounds of the orphanage became Natalie's world. She went to school there. She ate there. She slept there. It was a world of lost children. The workers, for the most part, were mean and heartless. Some even beat her and the other children for the slightest infraction.

"They would say to us, 'I don't have to put up with you. You will never amount to anything because your mom was a drunk. You are a worthless orphan and will never amount to anything.'

"I cried many tears, especially when the teachers would say, 'One day your kids will be living here.' I would pray to God, 'I don't want my kids to be here.' I knew of girls who left the orphanage a few years ago, and their kids were here—it was like a circle that never breaks. I didn't want that to happen to me and my kids."

At night Natalie could not sleep because she was constantly hungry, longing for more than the thin sweet cereal served on a rusty tin plate they were given every day for dinner.

On Saturdays, when Natalie didn't have school, she started a routine. Every single weekend, she'd get up, dress as carefully as she could, and, after breakfast, walk down to the brown iron gate at the entrance of the orphanage. From there, she could see any buses coming down the road long before they were on the grounds.

> She hadn't even walked down the hall to see Natalie.

"I would stand there and wait for my mother to come and visit. All day I would stand there, looking up the road, breaking only for a quick lunch before rushing back to my post."

Soon, Natalie's best friend, Dasa, started to join her at the gate in hopes that her mother would come, too. Other parents came to visit their children, but never Natalie's or Dasa's.

"But we would stand there in the rain or the snow and watch the road, just in case," Natalie remembers. "By the end of the day, we would start making excuses for them. Perhaps they didn't have the money for the bus. Or it was too cold. Maybe they were sick."

One day years later, after spending countless Saturdays waiting by the gate, Natalie learned that her mother had come to the orphanage with her new boyfriend to see his children, to bring them toys and candies. She hadn't even walked down the hall to see Natalie.

Natalie told me that the day they were put out on the bench, she was trying to think of a way to survive. Her grandmother was still alive, but still too poor to even feed herself. There was no work in her village, but what choice did she have?

The day she was invited to come and live at Stella's House was the greatest day of her life... up to that point.

"We had heard about Stella's House, but it sounded like a dream too good to be true. I was afraid to even pray I would be invited.

"I remember when I first opened the door to Stella's House," she shared recently. "It was so clean, I started to take my shoes off, scared I would mark the floor. But everyone said, 'It's okay, come in; you are welcome.'"

Before then, Natalie told me that she had never felt welcome anywhere in her whole life.

"I started to cry as they showed me my room and my bed. It seemed too nice for me. I was only an orphan. Everyone was smiling. They gave me clothes, not just one set either. New clothes! Shoes that fit! Even pajamas. I had never owned a pair of pajamas."

A few months later, I had the joy of leading her in the sinner's prayer. "When I learned that Jesus loved me enough to die for me, I started to weep. I had never known a love like that," Natalie said.

"Now I want to speak for other orphans. They have a voice, but no one wants to hear them," she told me before we even named our ministry Stella's House.

Her best friend, Dasa, was also chosen by the girls to come to Stella's House.

Looking at Dasa's long, silky blonde hair, it is hard to picture her trying to look like a boy. But she did. While more reserved about her feelings, she told me, matter-of-factly, the overview of her story.

"When my mother got pregnant, my father told her that he wanted a son," she remembers. "If she gave birth to a girl, he would leave. My mother blamed me for years that he was gone, so I tried to act like a boy."

Her early years were spent crammed into a miserable small house with not enough to eat and very little love.

"My earliest memory is of being marched outside with the other kids," she told me. "It was very hot. My uncle threatened to hit us if we didn't kneel down on some hard, dry kernels of corn while he screamed at us. He was angry at my aunt for leaving us alone with him."

Every day was filled with fear for the tiny blonde girl. Once her uncle threw scalding water on her cousin. She slept in the bed with the other children and awoke many nights to the terrifying sounds of her mother or one of her aunts being beaten. "Please don't kill me," they would beg while the children cowered in their beds.

It was a blessing to the kids when her uncle was arrested as a thief and sent to prison. Life had just started to seem better when suddenly, the other adults decided to leave the country for a "better life." Her mom was left with four kids and nothing to feed them.

"I don't remember what we ate, but we were hungry all the time," Dasa remembers. "I never felt like my mother loved me. No adult paid any attention to us. We were supposed to stay still, be quiet, and stay out of the way."

Dasa's mother finally followed her sisters and made a few attempts to find work in Russia. The children were left alone in the house for weeks at a time. Every few days one of her older cousins would come by with some rice to keep them alive.

"I would go in my mother's room, to her closet, and pull out her clothes and try to catch the smell of her," Dasa told me. "I wanted her to come home so badly."

Then, Dasa received word that her mother had been in a car accident and was clinging to life in a coma. Her mother survived, but her relatives decided to put all the children in the orphanage.

"Nothing was very different in the orphanage," Dasa remembers. "I was still hungry all the time. I was alone. No one cared for me. It was the same pain."

Now, instead of a drunken uncle, Dasa had to deal with mean staff workers who would tell her, "You are nothing. An orphan is less than nothing. You will never be anything."

After nine miserable years in the orphanage, it was almost time for Dasa to leave—not that she had anywhere to go. She had heard that we had opened Stella's House, but she didn't think there was a place for her there. Dasa knew of us because we had been bringing the Christmas gifts to her and the others for years.

> After that she understood that she mattered to me and to her heavenly Father.

But she was painfully aware that there were 17 other girls who would age out of the orphanage at the same time. She told me later, "I was afraid to even pray. I felt I had no chance because my mother is still alive. Plus, I had learned to never trust anyone. Everyone had failed me. How could I trust you?"

Months later, long after we had taken her into our care, we were talking, and I said to her out of the blue, "You know what? I don't like boys. I really don't like them. Girls are special." I saw the light come into her eyes. A sparkle. After that she understood that she mattered to me and to her heavenly Father.

Since then, Dasa has blossomed into an outstanding young woman of faith. She is a leader among the girls, excelling at her studies, with big plans for her life.

"One day I want to open Stella's Houses in Africa or other countries," Dasa said. "Everywhere the government runs orphanages, they need Stella's Houses. I want to spend my life helping others the way you helped me."

We were only able to save three that day. One of the 15, we found later when a bed opened up. The rest? I have no idea where they are, what happened to them.

As sad as that makes me, I am grateful that we have been able to bring in many more since then. Each of them has a unique story. Let me share Valentina's story with you. Her experience is unlike any of the others'.

She was just a normal little girl being raised in a rare Moldovan middle-class family. When she was seven, her dad came toward her, and she could tell he was drunk.

Out of nowhere, he said, "You are adopted." Valentina was crushed. How could that be?

He went on to tell her that she was born into a very poor family, the youngest of six. Her mother died when she was only one, and her father gave her up because she was so young and needed more attention than he could give her.

"He told me that they had been unable to have children of their own, and they were glad to adopt me. They always treated me with love, and I never thought I was not really part of the family, but it felt different for me after that," she told me.

When her mother was 53, she found out that she was pregnant. Valentina was 14 and was excited that she would finally have a sibling. But nine months after her brother was born, Valentina's dad found out that he had gastric cancer. He was the wage earner in the family, and suddenly he was too sick to work.

Valentina's mother had to work in the field just to provide food for her children. She had high blood pressure and worried all the time about money. When Valentina was 18, she graduated from high school and left to go to college, but she lived on only $20 a month.

"One day there was a holiday in Moldova, and I had come home," she remembers. "I was outside with my friends, and there were traditional dancers in costume, music—it was one big celebration. In the middle of the festival, an ambulance rushed by, going toward my house."

Valentina dashed home, following the ambulance as best she could. When she got there, her aunt and uncle told her that her mother fell as they walked in and had been unconscious ever since.

> She told me, "God gave me the ability to dream again. I have the power to do better and go ahead with life. I am able to put my trust in the Lord."

"I was so scared," Valentina said. "Mom was hardly breathing. I started to scream; I had never seen Mom like that. She died in my arms on the way to the hospital."

Valentina cried as she remembered the feelings that overwhelmed her in the ambulance. "It was a nightmare," she said through tears. "I had a five-year-old brother, my father was very ill, and I had no job. How would we survive?

"I could not stay in school. I had no money. I could not afford food. Then my cousin told me about Stella's House, and it was like heaven opened up. My aunt is caring for my brother for now while I finish school. I want to be a fashion designer, and my teachers say I have real talent."

I have seen this girl change dramatically. She knew a little about Jesus but told me that when she prayed, she didn't feel anything. Now she has an amazing personal relationship with the Lord and is witnessing like crazy. She told me, "God gave me the ability to dream again. I have the power to do better and go ahead with life. I am able to put my trust in the Lord."

These girls are my daughters now. And as long as I have breath in my body, I will protect them. All of them.

CHAPTER

THE GOLDEN
CORRAL TOUR

THE GIRLS ON THE bench, the ones we had lost into the darkness, underscored the need to expand Stella's House. We needed room for more girls, and we needed it quickly.

A little more than two miles away, we found property on a safe side street. On the two-acre lot stood the shell of a home that had never been completed, and on the neighboring lots were three other shells. If we could buy and finish them, we would be able to wall them off,

> I saw the light of promise in their eyes, in their gifts, in their drives.

providing an additional level of security, and provide a home for as many as 110 girls. But each of the shells was owned by a different family, and we hardly had the cash to buy all four at one time anyway. All we could do was buy one, complete it, and pray.

As we neared completion of the first home, I felt the Lord speaking to me through the girls. Many of them had brothers and cousins who had aged out at the same time as they had. These young boys were living on the streets, starving. Although they were not as much at risk for sex trafficking, there were countless reports of boys being enslaved and forced to work in construction in Russia under brutal conditions.

These boys were mine, too. They called me Dad. I helped raise them. I saw the light of promise in their eyes, in their gifts, in their drives.

So as Stella's first new houses opened, we converted the original building, two miles away, to Simon's House (named, of course, for my dad, the driving force behind my work). The day of the grand opening, my 78-year-old mother—the unsung hero behind everything my dad ever did—flew down from Scotland. She walked up the stairs, dressed to perfection, as always, with her perfect hair, her high-heeled shoes. She cut the ribbon to open the door and hung with care a large portrait of my dad in the living room.

As soon as the first Stella's House opened, we started on the second. Between the two Stella's Houses, a Simon's House, and work being completed as crises arose at other orphanages, plus our ongoing ministry in the United States and in Scotland, I often woke up from nightmares. My worst possible dream was that one day I would not have enough money to keep the houses going, and I would have to turn my kids out onto the street.

When I wasn't in Moldova, I was raising money at different churches every Sunday, filling in with midweek services and camp meetings anytime I was booked. It was grueling, exhausting, but I loved to tell the stories of these kids and how much they mean to me. Time and time again, I experienced the power of the Holy Spirit as I spoke, and somehow the funds were always there (though barely).

The members of some churches got so excited that they made missions trips to Moldova to see the girls, to hear firsthand where they had come from and what God was doing in their lives because of Stella's House. The results were always the same: Once people met these kids, they came to feel the way I did—protective, blessed, inspired, moved to tears.

I had to think that part of the reason it was so affective was that these girls (and boys) were not speaking through a translator. Most of them had taught themselves English, and they spoke with amazing clarity. Every raw emotion and feeling brought stories vividly to life, leaving nothing lost in translation.

Right after Christmas one year, I hosted one such group, of church ladies from North Carolina, at Stella's House. We settled around the leather couches in the living room, sipping tea as the girls took their places among us, on the floor all around us. The girls' smiles were infectious, and I grew quiet, as I had learned to do when someone new got a chance to meet and get to know "my kids."

> Like the process of adopting Andrew had been, the process of bringing the girls to the States was more complex and convoluted than I could ever put on these pages.

Gosh, I thought as I listened to the girls tell their stories, *if I could just get more people over here to hear them, I wouldn't have to do fundraising.*

I realized that I needed to bring some of the kids to the United States. They needed to tell their own story, to put a face and give a voice to the orphans in our care, the ones—like them—who would be prime candidates for sex trafficking.

Like the process of adopting Andrew had been, the process of bringing the girls to the States was more complex and convoluted than I could ever put on these pages. I knew enough about immigration and visas to the United States to know that I could apply for the girls to visit in the summer months, when school was out, but I could not predict who would be allowed to come or for how long. We started with the kids who loved the Lord, whose English was good, who showed interest in making the trip, and who had the maturity to be trusted with a new level of responsibility.

Everyone who made that list filled out an application for a visa. We hired a lawyer, chatted up everyone we knew at the Embassy. And then we waited.

Back in Alabama, I filled my days with more church visits, talking with at least one of the girls in Moldova every day. Everyone was waiting to find out who, if anyone, would be allowed to travel to the States for the summer.

I returned to Moldova in the middle of "mud season." It was almost Easter, and the winter winds had died down. It rained at least once a day, and the snowbanks were slowly melting. Water flowed from the hillside, and the soil had absorbed all that it could.

As much as I hated the snow, I hated the mud more. With every step, the mud would attempt to suck the shoes right off my feet, and if I somehow managed to get into the house with both still on, they were caked with thick dark mud that dried into what seemed to be brown concrete.

But I made it my practice to come to Moldova every year for Orthodox Easter, a week after we celebrated Easter in Alabama. It was a large and strange holiday in Moldova. Nothing like it is in America. Because kids often had strong emotions tied to the holidays from their childhood (good and bad), I always wanted to be there, like any loving father would. More importantly, I wanted to replace what they knew of Easter with what it really is.

On Easter morning in Moldova, families would get up early, go to Mass, then gather every member together, get in any car there was, and travel to the gravesides of dead family members.

Once in the graveyard, typically acres upon acres of graves marked with stone crosses, angels, and the like, the families would unpack for the day. There, right on top of the grave of Grandma and Aunt Sue or whomever, they would have a giant picnic and then start drinking wine, beer, vodka, or any other form of alcohol they could get their hands on.

Soon the children were all but forgotten as the boozing in the mud-covered cemetery continued. Evening would start to fall, and gravestones would begin to look dark and scary. A fire would be lit, more bottles would be opened, and the children would begin to huddle against one another from fear and for warmth. Until I met them, that was the only kind of Easter celebration these kids knew.

I loved to tell them the real Easter story, the story of Jesus, of His entrance into Jerusalem on Palm Sunday. The kids would hang on each word as I told them about the Last Supper, about when Jesus was arrested, and of His trial. Many would weep as I talked about our Savior being beaten and whipped until the flesh was torn away and His every bone and muscle was exposed. Then the cross, the nails, His mother at His feet.

With each telling, I would pause after I talked about the darkness that fell over the earth and our Lord simply saying, "It is finished" as He drew His last human breath.

Then came Sunday. I'd watch the girls' faces as I talked about the stone that was rolled away. He is risen! He is risen!

Yes, I loved to come on Easter and tell the story over and again. But this year, as we finished and conversations began to drift, the girls asked again about their visas. Would they be able to go to this country they had heard so much about? Could they meet the people who gave the money so that Stella's House could exist? Could they help Dad by telling their story? I didn't know, and I hated telling them I had no control of the decisions or the timing. All we could do is pray.

Two days later, I was sitting in the living room of Stella's One, going over the report card of one of the newer girls. I wasn't happy. Vio walked in with a funny grin on his face and caught my eye as I was finishing explaining why the grades are so important to her future, both for a career and for the government to allow her to stay with us and finish her schooling. Education remained the only reason they put up with us taking these girls in.

He pointed to an oversized beige envelope in his hand.

"Visas," he said simply.

I jumped up and led Vio into a side room where no one would overhear us.

"Let's see what we have," I said, holding my breath as I pulled them out. Quickly, I scanned over the documents and made two piles—one for the girls who had been approved, and another for the girls who had been turned down.

Half were approved for entry into the United States, while the others were turned down flat with no explanation at all.

After studying the visas more carefully, I noticed that in many of the cases, two of the applications were exactly the same, other than the name—same age, same year in school, same amount of time with us, from the same orphanage—yet one would be approved, and one, denied. It seemed as if someone had thrown all of the applications in the air as hard as possible. When the applications floated down and landed on the floor, the ones facing up were stamped with a YES, and the ones facing down were stamped with a NO.

Surely it was not that random, but it sure appeared that way. I braced myself to deliver the news. It killed me that I had to say no to some of them, but what else could I do?

> This became the first of many summer tours.

The girls were amazing when I shared the news. There were no tears from the ones who could not go, only hugs and shouts of joy for those who could.

As they celebrated, I broke away and called the office in Montgomery. We had only a few weeks to buy airline tickets, and it was vital that we all travel together. None of these girls would have a clue what to do if they were stranded overnight in Paris or Rome or some other gateway city. They needed their dad!

When we arrived in the United States, the Immigration officer asked each of the girls how long she planned to stay. Our girls all said, "Three months," knowing full well that the officer could refuse and write "Three weeks," or even "Three days," on the visa. It was nerve-racking, but all who made it into the States were approved for the three-month stay.

This became the first of many summer tours. I outfitted a used RV for the summer, and we set about across the country. We had a van filled with luggage, books, CDs, and other things we sold at churches, and my sons Philip Jr. and Andrew (now 28 and 20 years old) took turns driving. Chrissie and my two daughters, Melody and Lauren Ann (now 26 and 17 years old), rode with the girls and me in the RV.

At around midnight of the first day of our maiden tour, we stopped at an all-night diner to get something to eat. Except for a couple of highway troopers sipping coffee in the corner booth, the place was almost empty. A couple of the waitresses helped us push tables together, then passed out menus.

The chatter stopped as everyone stared at the menus in their hands. I was still deciding between the fish-and-chips (in Indiana, would any cook really know how to make fish-and-chips for a Scotsman?) and something they would be less likely to mess up—a hamburger, perhaps—when the waitress reappeared.

"What'll it be?" she asked, her pen poised over the order pad.

"Let the girls go first," I responded as I waved with my hand. "I'm still trying to decide. Galina? Constantia? Anybody? Just start."

Silence.

I looked over my menu at the girls. A dozen pair of bewildered eyes stared back at me.

"Come on," I said, my irritation barely contained, "just start."

It was Chrissie who finally broke the silence.

"Philip, I don't think they know," she said. "They can't read English and wouldn't know what these dishes are. Chicken fried steak? Cobb salad? Chicken and stuffing? They don't serve these things in Moldova, especially not in an orphanage."

And thus began what I like to call the "Golden Corral Tour." For as long as these girls travel with me, I have to find as many buffets as possible. Then they can see potatoes, green beans, roast beef…whatever, and make up their own minds what to eat.

> Each girl was remarkable in her own way.

But the meals were just the beginning of the adventure. The services, of course, were the highlight of the trip. I learned very quickly to give the microphone over as often as possible to the girls and let them share from their hearts.

Each girl was remarkable in her own way. The congregations would look at these girls—girls who looked so much like those in their own youth groups, in their own homes. Out of the girls' innocent mouths, the congregations heard about what it felt like to starve. To be beaten. Hated. Abandoned.

One of our stops was Branson, Missouri, where my dear friend Jim Bakker had a daily television program. Jim had been special to my family and me since back in the early '70s when he and Tammy Faye had been at *The 700 Club*.

Over the years, he had changed and grown as he walked through the valley, losing PTL, being publicly humiliated, being sent to prison for what seemed to be a life sentence, his wife divorcing him, his kids getting in trouble.

But like the Bible promises, He is a God who restores. Jim's lovely wife Lori was a delight, and his ministry was growing and thriving.

Jim began to weep as the girls shared their stories on his program. As the audience realized that, as terrible as it is, this is a solvable issue, Jim changed his earlier plans for the show.

"We want to help build the next Stella's House," he announced. "Will you help me?"

For most of an hour, we talked, testified, and Jim repeated the need. When the taping ended, we had no idea if the show would be successful, since it would not air for a few days.

I knew Jim's ministry was struggling financially, and, in fact, there were days when he seriously thought of retiring to some small cottage in the woods and forgetting it all. After all, he was 70 years old.

But quitting has never been in Jim's nature any more than it was in my dad's. When God said, "Do it," Jim did it, and his willingness to do God's work was evidenced all around the ministry he had named Morningside. The television program was just a small part of what he was doing. Perhaps the ministry with the longest-lasting impact will prove to be the school to train young people in evangelism and communications called Morningside Masters Media.

Bright, spirit-filled kids from all over the country were there, learning to run cameras and produce their own programs. They lived on the grounds, prayed together, worked side by side, and had become an amazing force for the kingdom. The girls of Stella's Voice quickly captured their attention. When we weren't on air, they were together, just being kids. Kids who love the Lord.

Galina had been suffering a lot that week, the pain in her eyes almost unbearable. After receiving permission to take her from Moldova to the United States for surgery on the tumor, a second X-ray in Alabama revealed that the tumor was gone. I insisted that they redo the scan, over the objection of the doctor.

"I know it seems like a waste of time, but trust me," I pleaded with him. "I'll pay extra for it, but please do it."

Finally, he agreed. The girls and I anxiously waited for the results. When Galina reached out and took my hand, she was smiling.

"I knew, because of how I was feeling, that something good was coming, and it did," she said.

She knew, before the doctor came back with the look of absolute astonishment on his face, that the tumor in her brain was gone, completely gone.

Although the tumor was gone, her eyesight was still blurry. She never complained to me, but I knew she was hurting. She was quieter than usual, more withdrawn, and I'd often catch her napping in the middle of the day.

Soon after, one of the girls from Masters noticed it, too, and began to ask pointed questions. Galina told the others the whole story, how she had suffered as a child not being able to see, but that there had never been a doctor to diagnose her, let alone even look at her.

"God can heal you," one of the students told Galina.

"Yes, yes," another agreed, and started sharing an amazing testimony of another healing that had happened at Morningside just weeks before.

Another student started quoting God's Word about healing: "Matthew 9:22 says, 'Jesus turned and saw her. "Take heart, daughter," he said, "your faith has healed you." And the woman was healed at that moment,'" the student told Galina, quoting the NIV. "And then there's James 5:14: 'Is anyone among you sick? Let them call the elders of the church to pray over them and anoint them with oil in the name of the Lord.' We want to pray for you, Galina."

The students gathered around Galina, placing their hands on her. The girls from Stella's House joined them. Boldly these children of God stormed the gates of heaven on behalf of Galina; boldly they entered into His presence. Many were praying in unknown tongues. One girl was singing a song of praise and worship, an angelic voice covering the prayers of so many gathered in His name.

A strange warmness settled over Galina as they prayed. The pain in her head ebbed. Everything became fuzzy when she blinked her eyes. After blinking again, she was amazed to find that she could see better, but through her glasses, things were out of focus. She took them off, and her vision was immediately clear. She was able to see better than she had ever been able to see before in her entire life!

She began to laugh and to cry, telling the others what she was experiencing. All prayer turned to praise.

"I felt like the heaviness disappeared," she later told me. "I felt reborn, like a new person. It's something I can't even explain. Even today, it's amazing, something you can't forget."

Hours later we pulled out in our RV, and the girls were strangely silent. We all kept stealing glances at Galina, who sat off in the back, still with no glasses, a look of complete serenity on her face.

Between trips and services, the girls literally became part of our family. We put beds up in the attic so they could all stay in our house. Chrissie made chore charts for them to take turns helping her cook, shop, clean, and handle other household chores.

Me? I was Dad. I made myself available as we were driving, as we waited for dinner, as we sat outside by the pool. It was in those hours that real healing began to take place for many of the girls. Details of their lives they had never told anyone came pouring out. Dreams. Fears. Questions.

Side by side we would sit for hours, one-on-one. Only God knows how many miracles happened in those visits.

By the time summer was over, I brought back to Moldova a very different group of girls from the ones I had brought to the States. They had all grown up. Their English was nearly perfect. They were grounded in their faith in a way that was breathtaking. They felt validated, important enough to travel, to take the message of the orphans to thousands and thousands of people. I was never prouder of them.

CHAPTER

THE BIGGEST
HAREBRAINED IDEA EVER

Seven years after we remodeled Cupcui, I stumbled upon this article online:

> Thirty-seven children live in the run-down state orphanage in the Moldovan village of Cupcui. But only one of them is actually an orphan. Many children in Moldovan state institutions have been placed there by their parents, motivated by grinding poverty, alcoholism, or other family problems and encouraged by a paternalistic state. A project spearheaded by UNICEF and the European Union to reunite children with their families, when possible, or place them in foster homes, hopes to change that.[*]

---

[*] Moldoveanu, Elena. "Effort to Place Orphans with Families Meets Surprising Resistance in Moldova." Web. 31 May, 2009. Radio Free Europe Radio Liberty. (http://www.rferl.org/content/Effort_To_Place_Orphans_With_Families_Meets_Surprising_Resistance_In_Moldova/1743564.html). 19 February, 2013.

The real story is this: The government was broke. Frankly, they don't like paying good money to feed and care for "worthless" orphans. So along came Child, Community, Family (CCF), an organization that caused grief by proposing that they close the Cupcui Orphanage and send the children back to their "loving families."

These "wise" officials went to the families and, one by one, asked them to take their children back. They all refused. Either they could not feed them or they had no interest in caring for them.

Seeing that they would get nowhere asking families to take their children back, the authorities reconvened around some self-righteous conference table, sipped some bad coffee, and looked at one another importantly.

It was around that table that someone came up with the single most harebrained idea in the nation's history: Let's bribe the families to take the children!

As crazy as that sounds, they all agreed, congratulated themselves on finding the perfect solution, and went home to their wives and vodka.

The next morning, back to the families the children went.

"I realize things are hard and raising a child is expensive. What if we were to help? What would it take for you to take your child back?" they asked. "How about 15 chickens? Maybe a kitchen table? A new front door? A goat? Would that make it easier for you?"

> I was furious beyond words.

One by one, the parents eagerly agreed to this mad version of *Let's Make a Deal,* and got whatever item they needed most in exchange for taking back their children. The parents took the children in, and then, as soon as the good people from CCF were out of sight, they put the kids back out on the streets.

Within days of closing Cupcui, the government was overwhelmed by incoming calls. One child's intoxicated uncle chased him across the yard with an ax. Two other children were abandoned in their home—simply left alone—while their parents took off for Russia. The children were found sleeping on the steps of the dark, closed orphanage with nowhere else to go. We heard stories of beatings, children who were starving to death, freezing cold, sleeping in the same bed as their parents.

I was furious beyond words. For one thing, we spent hundreds of thousands of dollars on Cupcui Orphanage only after the government had agreed in writing that the building would never be used for anything but a children's home for 25 years.

Aside from the ones we installed in the orphanage, there wasn't a single flushing toilet in the entire village of Cupcui. Although the orphanage was not as nice as I would have liked, it was far better than any of the homes to which these children had been sent back.

Beyond that, the closing of Cupcui was just plain stupid. What was the government thinking? If these families wanted their children or had the ability to care for them, they would not have been in the orphanage in the first place!

We were busy building Stella's House Two in hopes that by June 2010, I would not have to turn away a single girl who aged out of Cupcui or Straseni. Meanwhile, with no place to stay, those girls and boys in Cupcui—some as young as eight years old—were at risk for any number of dangers.

These were my kids! God gave them to me!

On my next trip back, I rushed to Cupcui Orphanage. The place haunted me. Empty. All the things we provided were stripped away. Windows were shattered, the place was covered in filth, and in the few weeks since it had closed, the orphanage had already fallen into disrepair.

I decided to call one of the local politicians. I learned quickly that my trip to Cupcui was by a divine appointment. At the very hour, the village officials were meeting to decide what to do with the building. All 39 of them were gathered in a room; 27 of them were Communist.

Moments later, I was banging on their door. With Vio as my translator once again, I carefully and calmly explained that I held a contract on that building. Before I remodeled the building, I reminded them, the government agreed that the building's purpose would be to house orphans for 25 years. Therefore, the decision they were gathered to make had legally already been made. They had no choice but to open it as a children's home again.

> Where had that
> come from?
> Was I mad?

As Vio communicated both my words and my attitude, I watched the faces. This was not good news to them. They had decided it would become a home for the elderly, and many of them had parents they planned to put there.

"We don't have the budget to reopen it," they told me.

I argued that the children were in danger, told them story after story. They didn't care.

"Okay," I said. The room was silent for a moment, and then, without thinking, I said, "Give it to me. I'll run it. Stay out of my way. I want nothing from the government but the key to the building and the ability to run it as I please."

Where had that come from? Was I mad?

I was in the middle of building Stella's House—the largest, most expensive project of my life—and I had just offered to take over a home for 130 kids. Vio, who has seen me spiritually jump off many cliffs in the decades we have known each other, looked at me in shock.

He slowly translated, still looking to make sure I wouldn't take it back.

My kids. I had to get my kids back. How could I do less?

I paced the floor as I waited for a decision regarding my proposal. Faces of my children danced in my mind. I had to find them!

The door opened, and Vio and I were ushered inside. They had taken a vote. Of the 39 individuals present, more than half Communist, 38 voted yes! I had myself an orphanage!

As I write this, I think about the faces of the children in our care today.

I thought of two sisters whom I loved dearly, Aurica and Cristina. I knew about their life before they were left at the orphanage when they were 11 and 12 years old....

Their father was an alcoholic and would come home drunk and beat their mother every night. They lived in constant fear that one day he would turn his wrath on them.

In self-defense, they would pretend to be asleep when he arrived and were forced to listen as their mother was beaten inches from where they lay.

Finally, they were taken to their maternal grandparents' home, where they lived for six years. The grandparents were kind, but the sisters' uncle lived there as well. They told me, "Uncle would scream at us and often beat us, using thick branches to whip against our bare legs.

"He hated children. He didn't like to hear us talk or play. We were just kids, and we wanted to play. But he decided to put us to work. If we didn't work, he would beat us some more."

Aurica and Cristina would be forced to work from dawn until dusk in the garden, in the field, and in the home. When their uncle could find no other project for them to do, he would ask neighbors if they had work for them, charging for their labor like they were slaves!

When their grandmother started to drink heavily, their world worsened; there was no protection from their uncle. And then one day, their grandmother fell, hit her head, and died. The only shield they had from their uncle was gone.

Without our help, where would my girls be today? Would their uncle be beating them again? Without us, there were few good options for these two wonderful girls. We knew we would follow wherever the Lord led to help them and the others like them.

CHAPTER

A CHURCH IS BORN

OVER THE COURSE OF 18 months, our small ministry went from having a single Stella's House with 25 girls to having two Stella's Houses with 43 girls.

With my pledge to run the orphanage at Cupcui, I had committed to open another home for orphans that would be home to as many as 130 children. My children.

It had been seven years since we had first found and completed work on the orphanage at Cupcui. Much of it surely needed to be updated. After bringing in consultants to assess the building, we found out that we'd need to invest $500,000 to turn this old, empty building into a home, a real home.

Overnight my world became a series of short nonstop trips back and forth between home and Moldova. I would go visit the girls and boys at Stella's House and Simon's House and oversee the building project. Then I'd fly home to preach and raise money for the ministry.

With every trip, I was more and more impressed with how the kids at Stella's House and Simon's House were maturing and growing as a family. Their spiritual growth was stunning. Being a Christian is not a requirement to live at Stella's or Simon's, but the first set of girls we took in instantly latched onto the Savior. Most of them had seen the *Jesus* film, had heard me share my faith when asked, and were just waiting for someone to lead them in the sinner's prayer.

As we brought in new arrivals, I noticed that the girls who had been living there for some time instantly befriended the newcomers, acting as "big sisters," helping them adjust to life at Stella's and sharing their newfound faith with the passion of a new believer. One of the girls was named Natalia. With all the Natalies and Natashas coming through our doors, it became confusing, so when the newest girl was welcomed into Stella's House, we called her by her last name: Sugar.

When she was very little, her mother was diagnosed with breast cancer. While she was in the hospital, Sugar and her brother were alone with their father. She told me, "He would beat us and never feed us. We would sneak over to the neighbors', and they would give us scraps of food. We had to hide this from him, or he would beat us."

When her mother finally came home from the hospital, both Sugar and her brother were glad. But their happiness didn't last long.

"That night, my father beat her, slamming her head against the wall. There was blood everywhere. Then he turned on my brother. My brother was very bruised from his last beating, so I tried to stop my father. He back-handed me, causing me to fly across the room."

Then, her father grabbed a butcher knife. Sugar panicked and ran out into the cold night air.

"He threw the knife at me, and if I had not slipped on the ice, I would have been stabbed," she remembers. "My brother and I stayed outside all night in the snow because we were too scared to go back inside."

When she was five, her dad became sick, turning yellow, then orange from liver failure. His death was quick and painful. After he died, Sugar's mother took her and her brother to their grandmother's and never came back.

"Grandmother had no food to feed us, so she took us to stay at the monastery with the nuns. When she could not pay them, they put us out on the streets."

Two years later, Sugar was placed in the huge orphanage at Straseni.

"I used to sit in the corner of the bedroom and cry," she said. "I would dream of running away. Other times I would dream that my mother would come and find me and take me away. But I never saw her again."

Although Sugar had been around some nuns when she was little, she never saw any love from them. "Just fighting," she said. "They were always fighting."

It wasn't until Sugar arrived at Stella's House that she saw the love of Christ in action. The residents of Stella's House were anxious to share their faith with her. It was as natural to these "on fire" new believers as telling them how to operate the washing machine or cook soup on the stove.

> No one was ever forced to go, but every single girl went every week.

I would come in for one of my visits unannounced and find a few reading their Bibles together or singing praise songs on the living room couch. Every Sunday, we took several trips with the vans to bring all of the girls to church. They were always excited to go; it quickly became the highlight of the week. They were anxious to grow and to learn.

They loved the worship, the study, and the people. As orphans, they never quite fit in in the community, but they loved it; it was like nothing they had ever experienced.

No one was ever forced to go, but every single girl went every week.

Then something happened that made me proud. One Thursday night, the girls surrounded me and asked, "Dad, this Sunday, instead of going to church, can we have church here at Stella's House, and you preach?"

Of course, I said yes! Then another said, "I have an idea! Let's invite our friends from school!"

The others piped up their approval of the idea. "Yeah! Let's do that!"

I looked at their pretty faces and almost cried. What these girls were suggesting would require them to admit to those friends that they were orphans.

From the time they came to Stella's House and started new schools, there was no reason for the girls to tell anyone, especially their new friends, that they were orphans. No one knew. My girls dressed as well as, and sometimes better than, their friends at school and shared the same quality of life.

But to share Jesus' love with others, they were willing to risk being hated, outcast, and scorned yet again. For the first time in their lives, they were being treated as equals—but they would willingly give that up in the hope of leading their friends to Jesus.

> That day we had 110 people in church. Sixty were visitors. Fifty-six asked Jesus into their hearts as Lord and Savior!

I was overwhelmed at the commitment to Christ these girls were showing. And what an honor for me to preach to their friends. I could not wait until Sunday!

All day Saturday, the girls were busy setting up more than 100 folding chairs in the basement—also the girls' recreation room—of Stella's Two, crafting a makeshift pulpit, and hanging some art to remind us that we were "at church."

Early Sunday morning, about twenty minutes before church, I noticed a group of the girls running out the door and up the snow-covered street. I called to Dasa, "Where are they going? It is almost time for church."

"They are going to meet the bus at the bus stop up the hill and welcome their friends to church and our home," she explained.

I looked out the window, and she was right. They were hugging their friends like they had not seen them in years, taking their hands, leading them to Stella's House.

Let church begin!

That day we had 110 people in church. Sixty were visitors. Fifty-six asked Jesus into their hearts as Lord and Savior!

But something else happened that day: A church was born. The kids decided they wanted their own church and that one Sunday a month would be designated as Salvation Sunday.

Today, they preach every Sunday and lead praise and worship. They lead new believers through the sinner's prayer and invite them to Bible study all under my careful supervision and encouragement.

These kids, many of whom had never heard the name Jesus until they arrived at Stella's House or Simon's House, are evangelists on campus, so on fire for Jesus that they cannot contain it.

Anna is one of the girls miraculously transformed by this church. I remember when I first laid eyes on her. She was sweet, but quiet—so very quiet (very different from the other Ana).

Though stunningly beautiful, with her tall, thin frame and long blonde hair and haunting blue eyes, she quickly faded into the background of Stella's House, opting to remain in her room and away from the other girls. I suppose I wasn't surprised by her behavior, as her past was marred with fear and uncertainty.

From the other girls, I learned that when she was only a little girl, Anna watched her father beat her mother mercilessly. Blood spattered against the walls and trickled down her mother's forehead while he continued to violently abuse her. Finally, she collapsed on the floor, and her father stopped, satisfied with the results.

"You better get to a hospital," he sneered through his clenched teeth. And with that, he returned to bed.

Three days later, Anna's mother died, never having seen a doctor.

Anna was left at an orphanage the next day. Her father visited occasionally, and every so often, a family would support her in their home for the weekend.

"I was placed with one family that made me work the farm all day, milk the cows, and babysit their children," Anna later told me. "When I was older, I returned home to my father during the summers when the orphanage closed. He made me cook and clean, but I didn't know how to perform the tasks, so he beat me."

Needless to say, Anna was thrilled when summer "vacation" ended, and she could return to the orphanage. As she grew up and became a teen, Anna began to hear about Stella's House. To the shy, lonely girl, it seemed too good to be true. She ignored the stories, believing them to be rumors.

One morning, at around 2:00, a knock on Anna's door alerted her of a phone call. Curious, she picked up the phone, only to hear her father's heavy, unsteady breathing. He was drunk.

"What are you doing?" he asked in his drunken stupor, his gruff voice and slurred words seeping through the phone.

"Sleeping," Anna whispered, rolling her eyes, just wanting to get off the phone and go back to bed. "You?"

"Watching porn," he answered matter-of-factly. "Do you know what that is?"

Anna remained silent. Her father slowly began to explain in graphic detail each image that appeared on the screen. Finally, he broke the X-rated play-by-play.

"You keep your body pure for me," he told Anna, "because when you get out of the orphans home, you and I will be making babies together."

Anna dropped the phone on the floor, horrified, her stomach turning. She was overwhelmed with fear. She would age out of the orphanage at only 16 years old—mere months from then—and she had nowhere to go but home to this monster.

The next morning, during her first class, she confided in a teacher about what had happened. The teacher heard her story, appeared bored, and finally responded, "What a liar. Get out of my classroom, you slut."

Soon after, Anna confided in a friend, a resident at Stella's House, who returned to the house later, shared this frightening story, and begged me to take Anna in.

> She turned 16 that very day.

"Please, can we find her a bed? Is there a room?" she pleaded.

My heart ached for this child. I had to save her before her father destroyed her forever. At the time, a bed had freed up, and I was able to quickly move Anna into the shelter of our home. She turned 16 that very day.

The girls at Stella's House became very protective of her. But they also demonstrated unconditional love, turning the other cheek when she acted out or melted in emotional tears or rants.

As she was ready, they shared the love of Jesus Christ with her, how He gave His life to save her own, and how she is a precious daughter of the Most High King. Though skeptical at first, she came to accept the Lord as her personal Savior.

My heart leaps with joy when I pass by her room and see her sitting cross-legged on her bed, quietly reading the Scriptures. Although she is terribly shy, she is warming up to the others. It takes time to learn how to trust again—but we have that time at Stella's House.

A number of my kids are now leading worship, teaching, and preaching. Nadia, Irina, Dasa, Johnny, Artiom, Maia, and Sylvia each are growing into dynamic leadership positions and rearing up new believers who will one day take their place when they graduate.

Imagine what these kids can do in Moldova. I know in my heart they will change the country forever.

CHAPTER

CUPCUI REBORN: PROVIDENCE HOUSE!

DESPITE THE WORK WE had done at the orphanage in Cupcui over the past seven years, there was still much work to be done before I would feel comfortable bringing "my kids" there, especially after it was stripped and emptied of its contents.

The building felt like an empty cave. All that remained was the plumbing. We were forced to do a complete reconstruction. Every weekend I sent Galina and some of the other kids from Stella's and Simon's out to work with the hired help to clean and repair.

> The building felt like an empty cave.

Galina never said a word to me, but she hated every single minute she was there. The place haunted her, revealing old scars she thought had healed long ago. Because she was between school sessions, I had her out there during the week, supervising the workers—including some of the very women who had been so mean to her as a child. She was their boss.

One day, a former orphanage worker came to the door, and Galina stopped her in her tracks. Galina stood as tall as her five-foot-one-inch frame would allow and looked the woman right in the eye. "You can't come in. You are not allowed in here."

The woman sneered, "Who do you think you are? You are nothing but an orphan. I know where you came from!"

Galina stepped closer, "I am in charge here, and you are leaving now!" And the woman left.

Still, being there was painful. "I could not wait to leave and return to the safety and love of Stella's House," she told me. "The days just dragged on. I wanted to get the orphanage opened so I could leave."

Meanwhile, we were getting pressure from the government to open at once—there were children whose lives were literally in danger. Every day counted!

The officials took me to the "home" of two little girls. I say *home* because there was a roof and a floor, but the door did not close, and all the windows were broken. It looked like a small abandoned hut that should have been condemned.

Every piece of furniture was broken. Dirty dishes covered the small counter. Bits of dirty, ragged clothing and random junk littered the floor.

It was so cold standing in that house that my teeth rattled. If there was a bite of food to be found, I could not see it. In their coats, boots, and mittens, the children huddled against the inner wall.

When their mother noticed us, she began to wail, thinking we would take away her children. The child advocacy worker had told us that their father was a drunk and had vanished a few weeks before. The woman was disabled and could not work. The children were suffering from malnourishment; their health and schoolwork reflected it.

I could not yet take the girls. The reconstruction was complete, but the government officials had decided that they were not finished writing the regulations for running the home. I was outraged. In the time it took me to totally rehabilitate that building, they could not finish writing a single paper? Not when they had been running orphanages since the country was born?

Finally, in April of 2011, we opened our doors. Once again, I had Galina to help with transitioning the first few children.

The first child we picked up was a 10-year-old boy named Steopa. He had not seen his mother in a long time, but he knew she was a prostitute, and his dad had kicked her out of the house years ago.

His dad worked a lot, and his sister had cared for him since he was six. She was only eight years old at the time. They were left alone at home for weeks at a time. As of now, Steopa's father is in Italy looking for work, and no one knows if he will ever be back.

As traumatic as that sounds for a child, Steopa was happy from the moment he walked through the door of Providence House. He smelled food to eat, and it was warm.

Next to arrive at Providence House was a 14-year-old girl named Pasa, Steopa's older sister. In spite of the fact that their mother "turned tricks," they both remembered her as a kind woman, but she and their father fought all the time, hitting each other and scaring the children.

There was never any food in the house. "I love the food here," she told me. "And everyone is so nice to me. I feel loved, and I like hearing about Jesus. He gives good things!"

They had two other siblings: seven year-old Liuvmile and six year-old Victoria. They had both spent the last three years sleeping on a bench with their mother. There was not a bed in the house, there was no food, and their parents cursed them daily for being born.

Finally, Liuvmile asked, "Why did you make me if you did not want me?"

The second day she was there, the youngest girl asked Galina why she was so nice to them. "My mother and dad hated me. Why do you like me?" she asked.

Galina had to turn away so that Liuvmile would not see her cry. Later she said to me, "Dad, I cried that night because when I lived here as a child, there was no one to be nice to me, no one to make me smile."

Then I got another crazy call. There was a girl with a baby, and they had nowhere to go. Against all odds, this girl had her baby. Her boyfriend left her because she would not abort. She had to hide from her family for fear they would physically force her to have an abortion. When they couldn't find her, they cut her off financially in a final attempt to make her change her mind.

Now she has a one year-old baby and has survived months living in sheer poverty. When she came looking for help, all she owned were a few baby things and her clothes from high school.

"My baby never did without. I was hungry. I had nothing. But my baby is all that matters," said Tatiana, a brown-haired beauty. "But I have been so scared, so hungry, so alone. Before I had the baby, I was in school, studying to be a doctor. I worked two jobs. One started at 4:00 a.m.; the second one ended at 6:00 p.m. Then I went to school."

She was at work early in the morning a few days into her seventh month when her water broke, and her life changed. For seven days, she suffered in labor while doctors did nothing.

"I have never been more alone in all my life. All I could think about was that my family said they never wanted to see the baby or me. I brought them shame. My boyfriend was already involved with someone else."

For two weeks after giving birth, she could not walk or sit. Her breast milk dried up due to the stress. She cried all day as she rocked her baby.

As soon as her family heard of the birth, they tried to come and forcibly take Tatiana away and leave her baby behind. She had to physically fight them off, grab her baby, and hide out in the woods in the dead of winter.

Where would they have taken her? What would have happened to her...to her baby? I shudder to think.

We didn't open Providence House to take in single mothers, but how could I say no? These two were at terrible risk, living in horrific conditions. Here at the home, there were two rooms, a living area, and a bedroom that were perfect for this tiny family to live within our family.

That first night, Tatiana wept with tears of joy with Galina. "Dad," Galina told me, "we were up until 4:00 a.m., talking about the Lord. She can't get over the fact that someone cares enough to provide a way for her to get on her feet and raise her baby."

"I feel safe for the first time in so long," Tatiana told me during the first week she was at Providence House. "I am at peace. I want to know more about this Jesus, who made it all possible."

As more children arrived, Galina stayed at Providence House.

"Something happened to me I never would have thought," she said. "I do not recognize myself. I love these kids so much, I don't want to leave. Ever. If I go to Stella's House for a few days, I find myself wondering, *What are the kids doing now?*"

Stela, another resident of Stella's House, feels the same way. When she was just a baby, her father sat on her face in an attempt to kill her.

The abuse continued for years, until she was transferred to an orphanage when she was ten.

"I was relieved, but I was also scared my dad would kill my mother," she said.

Although living in an orphanage is never easy, it is even more difficult for girls Stela's age.

"I was ignored by the other girls at the orphanage because they didn't like me," she said. "They already had their friends and didn't take easily to a newcomer."

Many times, Stela just wished she could return to the abuse at home rather than be subjected to the taunting, jeering, and physical abuse from other girls.

It was the girls at Stella's House that gave Stela the first hope she ever had. "They came and played with us and talked about Jesus. When I turned 16, I asked about Stella's House, hoping I could live there one day.

"I was afraid what would happen to me if I could not go to Stella's House. So many girls have disappeared," she told me.

Stela has blossomed at Stella's House. Her greatest joy? "Now I go back to the orphanage and help other children. I am so very grateful."

CHAPTER

THE ORPHANS' DAD

I AM THE ORPHANS' DAD.

The number of girls and boys that I call my own increases almost daily. They complete their education, move on as adults, find their own apartments and jobs, and begin lives with real futures. But they are still my kids, as much as your grown children are yours. I see and hear from them all the time, offer advice, rejoice in their victories.

> June 1 marked National Children's Day in Moldova.

And meanwhile, there are new orphans coming to Stella's House, Simon's House, and Providence House all the time. Their stories are tragic, like those who have come before them, but different.

June 1 marked National Children's Day in Moldova. On that fine warm day, there were parties across Moldova, celebrating her children, that included music, dancing, balloons, and sweet treats.

For the 16-year-olds living in orphanages, it was the beginning of the end. They finished cleaning and painting their rooms. The next day, they were sent away. Not one soul cares what happened to them after that—if they have something to eat, if they have a place to sleep, if they are safe.

No one knows, and no one cares if they are even alive after they leave the orphanage. Who would know?

If you care about this evil called sex trafficking, an industry that is larger and safer than illegal drugs (some say as much as $44 billion a year), this is where you must start.

There is no larger pool of vulnerable, easy-to-obtain, fresh-faced girls than the orphans of Moldova. This small nation is the engine for sex trafficking for all of Europe, but I didn't get involved because sex trafficking was suddenly the cause to fight. I got involved because these girls are my own; I am their father.

Years ago, I had a meeting with the United States Ambassador to Moldova, Michael D. Kirby. We sat in his downtown office, and he said, "Philip, the Moldovan girls who are naive enough to get unknowingly into the cars of sex traffickers are beaten, raped, and stripped of their passports within 24 hours. They are taken illegally to places like Turkey, Saudi, and Italy."

> There are thousands and thousands of orphans in Moldovan institutions today. Hundreds are aging out in June. More than half are girls. Where will they go?

These girls are sexually and physically abused over and again by people trained to break the spirit of these girls, until they are ready to do anything for anyone just for the pain to stop. Then they are sold, as often as 30 times a day, to any stranger with a few dollars. If they turn up pregnant, they are beaten again. If they don't miscarry, they are forced to have an abortion. Over and over, they are used, with few living beyond a few years.

There are thousands and thousands of orphans in Moldovan institutions today. Hundreds will age out in June. More than half are girls. Where will they go?

At this writing, the 50 beds at Stella's Voice are filled, as are the 15 at Simon's House and the 48 at Providence House. A handful of girls will graduate from Stella's. About the same number will age out of Providence and need to come to the city to finish their education.

Beside Stella's One and Two, construction is under way for the most ambitious and expensive project of my life. Three buildings are rising to meet our most immediate challenges. On either end will be another Stella's House, each designed to offer a home for 30 more girls, 60 in all. In between the two homes will be the heart of the campus, a church building that will seat 300 for worship.

When we started the project, we bought two shells—half-built houses that by God's design were next door to the first two Stella's Houses. We had a budget and a plan approved and had raised enough to begin the project.

> You, too, can help us stop sex trafficking in Moldova!

Then the enemy came against us. Neighbors started complaining about housing all those young girls so close, compromising their common sewer lines. Finally, the government got involved—which is never good. It demanded that we remove the shells that were standing and start over completely, adding hundreds of thousands of dollars to the budget.

I was discouraged but never doubted what God had called me to do. Together with my Christian friends in the United States, Canada, and the United Kingdom, we are building more beds, and more girls and boys will be prevented from being a part of the largest population of slaves history has ever recorded.

You, too, can help us stop sex trafficking in Moldova! With your help, we can provide a safe, loving, Christ-filled home for aged-out orphan girls in Moldova. Next June, another group of innocent girls will be sent away from the state-run orphanage. Help us do more, save more. Help us to build a place for them and give them a bright future.

EPILOGUE

IT WAS THE FINAL day of the 2012 tour. For months, a group of Stella's House girls had crisscrossed the United States with me in our RV, talking to churches and schools and nagging me to stop at every Golden Corral along the way.

The last day of August was pleasant and warm in Montgomery; the stifling heat of summer was finally leaving us. I sipped my morning tea and looked out the front window of our bedroom. Roses of every color bloomed in the careful beds Chrissie had nurtured, and yellow and purple pansies danced in the slight breeze.

The activity in the house was greater than on most early Friday mornings, with the girls and Chrissie up at dawn, hauling last-minute things into boxes and running out the door. By noon, they were all back, but no one was talking to me. The girls dashed straight up to their rooms in the attic, chattering away like clucking hens, laughing and screaming.

This day was different from any other I had experienced on the last day the girls would be in America. Typically, there are nonstop tears and moans of, "It's our last day in America... our last night at Dad and Mom's... I may never get to come back... I don't want to leave." But today, the girls were far too busy to stop and chat with me and too focused on the night ahead to shed tears or even think about the trip back to Moldova the next day.

I felt strangely alone. Everyone other than me had tasks to do. Andrew hadn't been seen since the night before. Philip Jr. was busy with his video crew. Chrissie was the ringleader of the event, managing the girls, the family, and everything else. She had Melody and Lauren Ann off handling last-minute errands, but she was in the kitchen checking off her list, oblivious to the fact that I had walked in the room. I watched her with her mouth set, that comforting determined look on her face. She'd get it all done, pull it all together; of that, I had no doubt.

Late that afternoon, I went back to the lonely master bedroom and dressed alone. I knew I shouldn't have felt sad and lonely, but I did. Chrissie had left my suit out on the bed, along with the shirt and tie she had picked out to go with it. Dressing with care, I let my mind wander, as all parents do. Where had the years gone?

> How could I not fall in love with her?

I thought back to the day I'd first seen Chrissie, nearly 40 years before. I was in a church service with my dad, playing the accordion, singing praise and worship at the front. Out of the corner of my eye, I spotted a girl a bit younger than I, blonde and drop-dead gorgeous.

The fact was, at that time, I was carrying a torch for a girl who had broken my heart. I was not in the market for a new girlfriend. But I could not keep my eyes off this blonde. She was wearing a formfitting blue dress that showed off her perfect figure. Her hands and face were raised in praise, and she was radiant, glowing in her love for God.

How could I not fall in love with her?

She has put up with so much over the years being married to me. In the early days, I dragged her all over the countryside, living in a small motor home for years. Only after a year of traveling with baby Philip did the Lord open the door for us to have a home without wheels on it.

And then I was gone. She and Philippie were home in the double-wide trailer in Alabama as I traveled to any church that would have me. Melody came along and brightened our home with her sunny smile, and Chrissie was practically a single mother of two.

Now Philippie was married with two little ones of his own, and Melody had just gotten married a few months before.

I thought of Andrew, the bald little boy in the blue shirt at the orphanage, rocking back and forth, back and forth in his crib. Dirty, starving, looking at me with eyes so green, he took my breath away. Had it really been 21 years since we brought him home? And Lauren Ann, my baby, had just returned from Hillsong in Australia with the voice of an angel, all grown and stunningly beautiful.

By the time I finished dressing, I was alone in the house. I am never alone in the house, especially during the summer tour, and I didn't like the feeling of being in an empty house, so I hurried out to the comfort of my car. The drive to downtown Montgomery took about 20 minutes, and rather than click on the radio, I settled into the quiet. I thought of my Moldovan daughters, marveling at the changes I had seen in them this summer.

They were all waiting for me downtown. I stepped on the gas a bit and hurried down the road, finding an empty parking lot just across the street from my destination. It was in an historic part of Montgomery where the character of the buildings took me back to another time. I could imagine horses and wagons being parked out front of the stores 200 years ago, cotton being sold, shrimp from the sea, and yes, slaves.

Montgomery was one of the larger cities of the Deep South, and countless young men and women from Africa were bought and sold like cattle years ago. Yet for all our progress, there are more slaves today than at any time in history.

Inside the building, I headed for the fourteenth floor. When the heavy elevator doors opened, I was greeted by the smells of roast chicken and beef. My stomach rumbled, but I knew it wouldn't be time to eat for a while.

Stepping into the main room, I smiled. I had seen the room before, a large, plain room with simple decor. Chrissie and the girls had transformed it into a magical hall with white linen tables set to feed a crowd.

Silk flowers and ribbons adorned everything and everywhere I looked. It looked like something from a high-end magazine for the rich and famous, but it was all the handiwork of my girls.

The hour grew late, and I went looking for Chrissie. I hadn't seen her since morning, when she was still in sweats with her hair in a ponytail. When she turned around, I felt like I had felt so many years ago when I first saw her from the front of the church. There she was, my very own blonde beauty, standing before me in another formfitting blue dress. She was still stressing that everything was done and done perfectly, but I kissed her on the cheek, gave her a squeeze. Taking her arm, I led her back to the elevator, then to the rooftop of the building.

Moments later, the music started. Chrissie and I found our seats in the front row. Beside us were our guests from Moldova, Andrew's birth mother, Dana, and her husband, Vio. Both looked nervous and a little bit out of place. I hugged them, then draped my arm across the back of Chrissie's chair.

As I looked to the front, out walked Andrew. What a handsome young man he had turned out to be, still with those piercing green eyes, but with a presence and maturity that can only come from the Lord. He had become my right arm in ministry, using his college education to bring order to his dad's schedule and planning.

The image of him in his dark suit choked me up. The music changed, and the people around me stood as the "Wedding March" began.

Then, there she was in the doorway. Natalie. The little orphan girl who was one of 18 on the bench, just hours from being sent out into the streets. Natalie. The little girl who waited at the gate of the orphanage every Saturday for nine years, watching, waiting for her mother to come. But she never did. Natalie.

In her lacy white wedding dress, she looked like she belonged on the cover of a wedding magazine. Her beauty surpassed that of any model; her innocent face glowed. I tore my eyes from her and looked back at my son, my Andrew. The boy in the crib. The bald baby they told me there was no way I could adopt. No way.

And in my heart, I heard a song:

I know the Lord will make a way for me.
I know the Lord will make a way for me
If I live a holy life, shun the wrong, and do the right.
I know the Lord will make a way for me.

APPENDIX

Want to help? Here's what you can do:

1   **Make a donation.** Visit www.stellasvoice.org/donate to give a gift today.

2   **Join a prayer group.** Please pray for us as we pray for you. We encourage you to send in your prayer requests. Send your requests online at: www.stellasvoice.org/orphan-prayer-wall. Each will be prayed over, and lifted to the Father by name.

3   **Start a gift drive.** We need new coats, boots, toys, nonperishable food items, and much more.

4   **Take a missions trip.** Change a life while you change your own! Take a group to Moldova, and spend your days ministering to children and teens who have grown up hearing they are worthless.

5   **Start a fundraising page for Stella's Voice.** It is simple and will reach people who have never heard of Stella's Voice. Join us today, and make your voice even louder for the orphans in our care and for the ones we have yet to reach with the love of Jesus Christ.

6 **Share your page with family and friends.** Once you have created an account, add the link to your profile to help tell people about your fundraising.

7 **Share this book or our thirty-minute video (http://vimeo.com/31929615)** with your friends, family, and especially your pastor. Help us get invited to come and share. Some of our girls are in the States for most of the year. Their English is nearly perfect; their ministry gifts, beyond measure. Contact Andrew Cameron (yes, *that* Andrew) at acameron@stellasvoice.org.

8 **Give the orphans a better chance for a better life.** By doing any or all of these things, you are changing the lives of every orphan currently in our care and any orphan who comes into our care in the future.

Check out these products and help the orphans of Stella's Voice.

Wear The Mission!

Defend the Weak and the Fatherless

Let people in your life know you are part of Stella's Voice by ordering a T-shirt today. Begin a conversation about the horrors of sex trafficking, the plight of orphans in Moldova, but also the hope you have helped to share with these children—all by wearing a shirt!

Books

The Creativity of the Crisis

The God who upholds the universe by the Word of His power, the One who created everything out of nothing at all, knows exactly what He is doing when He allows crisis into our lives.

Stella's Sisters

Read the testimonies of five girls who were saved from a hopeless existence by a man and his ministry, Philip Cameron and Stella's Voice.

CDs

I Am Yours

A beautiful collection of praise and worship by the girls of Stella's Voice.

Website

To order any of the above products and more to help Stella's Voice, go to www.stellasvoice.org/store.

IF YOU'RE A FAN OF THIS BOOK, PLEASE TELL OTHERS

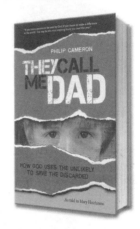

- Write a positive review on www.amazon.com.

- Purchase additional copies to give away as gifts.

- Suggest *They Call Me Dad* to friends.

- Write about *They Call Me Dad* on your blog. Post excerpts to your social media sites such as: Facebook, Twitter, Pinterest, Instagram, etc.

- When you're in a bookstore, ask if they carry the book. The book is available through all major distributors, so any bookstore that does not have it in stock can easily order it.

You can order additional copies of the book from my website as well as in bookstores by going to **www.stellasvoice.org**. Special bulk quantity discounts are available.

SPEAKING SCHEDULE

We'd love to share our stories with your organization. To schedule us, go to www.stellasvoice.org and click on the Book Stella's Voice today icon.